KT-483-860

fast cook

fast cook

Delicious low-calorie recipes to get you through your Fast Days

MIMI SPENCER

Photographs by Romas Foord

DISCLAIMER

If you are in reasonable health, short fasts (which will always, don't forget, include the Fast Diet's calorie allowance) should be fine. If you are on medication of any description, please see your doctor first. There are certain groups for whom fasting is not advised. Type 1 diabetics are included in this list, along with anyone suffering from an eating disorder. If you are already extremely lean, do not fast. Children should never fast, so this is a plan for over-18s only. Pregnant women should eat according to government guidelines and not limit their daily calorie intake. Similarly, if you have an underlying medical condition, visit your GP, as you would before embarking on any weight-loss regime.

Published in 2014 by
Short Books, 3A Exmouth House,
Pine Street, London, EC1R 0JH

10 9 8 7 6 5 4 3 2 1

Copyright © Mimi Spencer Limited 2014
Photographs © Romas Foord 2014
Design: Georgia Vaux

Mimi Spencer has asserted her right under
the Copyright, Designs and Patents Act 1988
to be identified as the author of this work. All
rights reserved. No part of this publication may
be reproduced, stored in a retrieval system
or transmitted in any form, or by any means
(electronic, mechanical, or otherwise) without
the prior written permission of both the
copyright owners and the publisher.

A CIP catalogue record for this book
is available from the British Library.

ISBN 978-1-78072-217-7

Printed in Great Britain by
Butler Tanner & Dennis,
Frome, Somerset, BA11 1NF

For my incredible shrinking father

9 | Introduction

19 | Fast Day favourites

45 | Lightning quick

73 | Warming and wonderful

99 | Fast-600 meals for men

125 | Simple sides

163 | Supper soups

180 | Calorie-counted index

186 | Index

WHITE CABBAGE, HARDBOILED EGG AND RED ONION, SEE P70

INTRODUCTION

A new Fast Diet cookbook

If you happen to find yourself at the Raw Bar at the One Canada Square restaurant in London, you'll see 'venison carpaccio and wild bass ceviche' on the menu, catering for 'the modern carb-phobic financier'. It's great to see that bankers are looking to cut back on carbs (many of them are on the Fast Diet, after all). But what if you're Jo Normal? What if, instead of finding yourself at the Raw Bar, you find yourself at the fridge door? Tired and grumpy on a Fast Day, with only minutes to spare and a whole lot of hungry going on?

Well, this book is for you.

It's for people who have read *The Fast Diet*, the book I co-authored with Dr Michael Mosley, and who are keen to introduce 5:2 into their daily lives. Soon after the Fast Diet took off last year, I wrote *The Fast Diet Recipe Book* to accompany it, a book designed to bring life, flavour and a bit of drama to the characterless landscape of low-calorie eating. It was aimed at people who, despite wanting to lose weight, quite liked to cook on a Fast Day. But this book, *Fast Cook*, is different. Fast Dieters have asked me for something served straight, no twist. They've asked for simple, practical basics. They want familiar favourites and hearty food, some of it in substantial man-size portions; a decent plate of proper nosh to leave them feeling satisfied and content, even when sticking to a Fast Day calorie quota.

In short, they wanted a support system for the 5:2 diet.

So here it is. Don't expect to fall off your seat in surprise. Most of the recipes here are cherished classics, rejigged to lower the calorie content but retain every bit of flavour. I've aimed for speed and convenience, with recipes that are easy to follow rather than game-changing – chiefly because a Fast Day necessarily demotes food to fuel. That, in part, is the point. So save the dreamy recipes for other days – there'll be plenty of those.

The Fast Diet: a quick recap

It may be radical, but the Fast Diet is also wonderfully economical with its rules. All you really need to know is that:

● You eat normally for five days a week and then, for two days a week, you consume a quarter of your usual calorie intake – around 600 calories for men, 500 for women. So, it is not total 'fasting', but a modified version. You won't 'starve' on any given day; there are still calories coming in

● You can do your Fast Days back to back, or split them. Michael tried both ways and found he preferred non-consecutive days, fasting on Mondays and Thursdays. So, it is not continual fasting, but intermittent

● Most people divide their calorie allowance between breakfast and an evening meal. You can, of course, skip breakfast and have a more substantial evening meal if it better suits your day. The key is to aim for a lengthy 'fasting window' between meals

● It does matter what you eat – plan your 500 or 600 calories by sticking, as the recipes here do, to the Fast Diet mantra: 'Mostly Plants and Protein'. That way, you'll stay fuller longer and get adequate nutrients in your diet

Do this, and you should experience the many benefits of Intermittent Fasting. These include:

● Weight loss of around a pound a week

- A reduction in a hormone called IGF-1, which means that you are reducing your risk of a number of age-related diseases

- The switching-on of countless repair genes

- A rest for your pancreas, boosting the effectiveness of the insulin it produces in response to elevated blood glucose. Increased insulin sensitivity will reduce your risk of obesity, diabetes, heart disease and cognitive decline

- A rise in the levels of neurotrophic factor in the brain, which should make you more cheerful... which, in a happy positive feedback, should make fasting more achievable

What, when and how to eat

It's worth spending a little time preparing for a Fast Day. It matters that you have at least thought about what you're likely to eat, simply to avoid the prospect of falling face first into the nearest chocolate fudge cake the moment hunger calls.

This book contains only recipes which would best suit an evening meal, since this is the time when inspiration is usually required. Breakfast on a Fast Day – if you choose to have it – is usually a simple affair based around the humble egg. A couple of eggs, scrambled and perhaps pepped up with tarragon or chives, seed mustard or chilli, clock in at around 200 calories and will really set you up for the day. Porridge – with pear and cinnamon, or berries and honey – will release energy slowly, particularly if you stick to jumbo oats. But it's supper which requires most attention; besides, it's the thing we Fasters look forward to most during the day. It's part of what gets us through.

For many people, speed and convenience are of the essence here. Get it fast from a packet or a bag if necessary. Open a tin. Poke about in the freezer. The following facts, tricks and tips should help you meet your Fast Day target.

PROTEIN: the body does not store protein, so we recommend that you boost the protein content of your diet on Fast Days, making it a greater proportion of your daily diet on just those days. That way, you benefit from its satiating effects (protein really does make you feel fuller for longer than carbs) and you will have adequate levels of protein at all times.

MEAT: cooking meat and poultry with its skin on will maximise its flavour and prevent it drying out, but don't eat the skin – it's a calorie trap. Also, roast or grill meat on a rack over a baking pan to allow excess fat to drip away. A griddle pan will channel fat into the grooves and away from your plate.

EGGS: a great start to a Fast Day, full of healthy fats, protein (all 9 essential amino acids), B vits and minerals. People who consume egg protein for breakfast are more likely to feel full during the day than those whose breakfasts contain wheat protein.

VEG PROTEIN: rather than rely solely on animal proteins, try to include vegetable protein on a Fast Day when you can. It's generally cheaper (and better for the planet too). Include nuts, mushrooms, tofu and pulses of all kinds. Legumes, such as lentils, chickpeas, split peas and beans, are excellent sources of plant protein and fibre, and rank low on the GI scale.

PLANTS: favour leafy greens over starchy veg. Steam, boil, blanch and griddle; don't overcook and don't fry. Roasting vegetables in a hot oven will caramelise their natural sugars; lightly spray with olive oil to stop them drying out.

DAIRY: use half-fat crème fraîche or low-fat natural yoghurt. Avoid butter on a Fast Day – it whacks up the calories. Certain cheeses are lower calorie than others: feta, for example, is made from sheep's milk and is a good source of protein, calcium and vitamin B12. Low-fat mozzarella is a handy staple in the fridge. Choose mature cheese instead of mild – its stronger flavour means you need less of it.

OILS AND FATS: I use cooking oil spray when I can – in general, most oil sprays provide about 15 calories per two-second spray. Otherwise, use olive oil, but sparingly. You only need expensive extra-virgin olive oil for salad dressings and drizzling; use standard olive oil for cooking. It's possible to avoid oil entirely when sautéing onion: simply use a non-stick pan and a splash of water instead of oil, and watch that it doesn't stick. Alternatively, use a silicon brush to apply oil to a pan and dab away any excess with kitchen paper. Most oils contain around 120 calories per tablespoon, so it's worth being particular about it when cooking.

CARBS: on a Fast Day? Not so much. The ones to avoid entirely are the fast-release blood-sugar spikers. Tropical fruits and juices are off-menu. As are white carbs. Slow-release carbohydrates – such as the jumbo oats in a bowl of porridge, or brown basmati rice – will, however, help fill you up and keep you going. If you find that a plate is naked without a carb fix, try shirataki Miracle noodles. Made of a water-soluble fibre called glucomannan, they have no fat, sugar, gluten or starch. What you'll need to add, though, is flavour.

Fast Day flavour... without fat

The recipes in this book are designed to add big bolts of flavour wherever possible. Here's how:

SPICE IT: herbs and spices should feature heavily in Fast Day cooking. Cumin seeds, cardamom pods, paprika, basil, coriander... they are central to a dish when fats are scarce. As a rule, use fresh herbs over dried as they tend to have greater flavour and more nutrients.

SPIKE IT: with mustard, onions, shallots, vinegar, chillies... anything that brings your fork to attention. There's much to be said, for instance, for the sweet joy of roast garlic: bake a whole head of it, sealed in foil with a splash of water, for 40 minutes. Once cooled, squeeze out the pulp and add to... anything at all. Green beans would be a good place to start. You may also like to embrace the Fantastic Five – lime juice, soy sauce, fresh ginger, garlic and Thai fish sauce – a combination known as nam jim which delivers a hit of flavour for very few calories.

BOOST IT: use sun-dried tomatoes or porcini in place of bacon or chorizo: both ingredients lend a smoky depth to a dish without the addition of careless calories. Paprika will perform the same flavour favour. Tinned cherry tomatoes have a sweeter, denser character than ordinary tinned toms, while tomato purée will up the ante in any tomato-based recipe (as will the merest pinch of sugar). Anchovies and capers will give a useful savoury, salty bite. And remember, when the world gives you lemons... make a salad dressing. Sometimes, just a squeeze of lemon is enough to jazz up a plate.

The Fast Day kitchen: what to have to hand

Get in the habit of having Fast-friendly food around – just enough to allow you to grab a quick meal when you're fasting and famished. Just enough to stop you dialling out for pizza.

IN THE FRIDGE
Eggs
Mackerel fillets
Smoked salmon
Half-fat hummus, low-fat yoghurt, half-fat crème fraîche
Feta, cottage cheese and low-fat mozzarella
Spring onions
Chillies
Fresh herbs
Non-starchy veggies: cauliflower, broccoli, peppers,
    radishes, cherry tomatoes, celery, cucumber,
    mushrooms, lettuce, sugar snaps, mange touts, salad
    leaves and a bag of young spinach

Carrots
Lemons
Strawberries, blueberries, apples

IN THE LARDER
Tinned tuna in spring water
Tins of beans – cannellini, borlotti, flageolet – and
  chickpeas
Tins of cherry tomatoes
Tomato purée
Garlic
Onions – red and white
Mustard – Dijon and English
Vinegar – balsamic and white wine; try balsamic spritzer
  on salad
Olive oil
Cooking oil spray
Spices, including cumin and coriander
Chilli flakes
Nuts – unsalted are preferable; eat with caution as they
  are generally high in calories
Pickles – guindilla, jalapeños, cornichons, capers
Marmite, Oxo cubes, stock cubes, miso paste
Sea salt and freshly ground black pepper
No-sugar Alpen
No-sugar jelly
Shirataki noodles

IN THE FREEZER
Root ginger – it is best grated from frozen
Stock – in empty (clean) soup and milk cartons
Soup – home-made or shop bought, in single portions
Blueberries (strawberries don't freeze well)
Peas

How the book works

Each calorie count is for a single portion, even if the recipe produces enough for 2 or 4 (or more) people. Recipes which produce larger quantities will generally be ideal for freezing. At the end of the book, you'll find a calorie-counted index to help you choose a dish that fits your calorie quota on any given day.

Where appropriate, recipes have 'serve with' options, and 'goes well with' suggestions from elsewhere in the book. Add the calories together to get your total for the meal. Most of the dishes are ideal for non-fasting family members too – simply add potatoes, rice or bread to make a more substantial plate.

A few words of Fast Day wisdom

Much has been written, and many stories shared, about the Fast Diet and how to succeed with the 5:2 approach. You'll find plenty of advice and tips on www.thefastdiet.co.uk. Here's my distilled version. A 5:2 stock cube, if you like:

● Drink plenty of water. Get into the habit of drinking a glass of water before and after Fast Day meals. And drink water when you feel hungry too (it really does help; the stomach is a simple beast). Supplement your water intake with herbal tea, black coffee, miso soup – but not juice, which can rack up the sugars. Diet Coke? OK, if it's the only thing that gets you through

● Remember, your aim is to secure a food-free breathing space for your body. So snack with caution: all calories count on a Fast Day, and your objective is to achieve as long a fasting window as possible. If you must snack, have berries, an apple, a carrot. Not a bag of Hula Hoops

● In any one week, work out a pattern that suits you: fast on a day when you are busy but not overly social; have breakfast as part of your calorie budget if that works for you – skip it if not. For lots more advice and personal takes, go to www.thefastdiet.co.uk

● Get a handle on hunger: the pangs will pass. We often eat because we're bored or emotional rather than actually hungry. Try to differentiate between the two. Real hunger won't hurt you – not for the mere handful of hours until you get your next food fix

● Stay calm. Going to 510 calories (or 615 for a man) won't obliterate a fast. While there's no particular 'magic' to 500 or 600 calories, do try to stick broadly to these numbers; you do need clear parameters to make the strategy effective in the medium term

● Stay positive. Don't be disheartened if you 'plateau' and don't lose weight in any given week; look at the medium term and remember the health benefits beyond weight loss – the real dividend is its long-term health gains, the prospect of cutting your risk of a range of diseases, including diabetes, heart disease and some cancers. There is also evidence that it will slow the ageing process and benefit your brain

Fast Day favourites

The classics. Only skinnier

We're all of us comforted by dishes we know and love, recipes we recognise and food that makes us nod in understanding, appreciation and anticipation. Our national repertoire includes the much-loved greats – the cottage pies and kedgerees – which have long been the culinary story of our land. Then there are the world-class classics: coq au vin, Thai curry, chilli con carne, spag bol… Most of us eat them day in day out, but these dishes can often clock up reckless calories. Here, then, I've taken a few of our favourites and slimmed them down to better suit a Fast Day. Fats, sugars and fast-release carbs are limited, while plants and proteins have the starring roles. You'll still find food you know, food you love. Just a darn sight skinnier.

CHILLI 3 WAYS...

Mexican black-bean chilli

144 CALORIES PER PORTION

Serves 4

Cooking oil spray
1 onion, finely chopped
2 courgettes, chopped
2 red peppers, deseeded and
  finely chopped
1 carrot, peeled and finely
  chopped
1 celery stick, chopped
1 garlic clove, crushed
1 red chilli, finely chopped
  (deseeded to taste)

½ tsp ground coriander
½ tsp ground cumin
1 400g tin cherry tomatoes
1 tbsp tomato purée
1 400g tin black beans, rinsed
100g frozen sweetcorn
75ml water
1 tbsp lime juice
Salt and pepper
Coriander leaves and natural
  yoghurt to serve

Heat oil in a large heavy-bottomed pan. Gently fry onion, courgette, pepper, carrot and celery on a medium heat for 5 minutes until softened. Add garlic, chilli and spices, stir and cook for a further 3 minutes. Stir in tomatoes, tomato purée, black beans, sweetcorn and water and simmer on a low heat for 20-25 minutes until sauce thickens. Stir in lime juice, season and serve with coriander and a spoonful of low-fat natural yoghurt.

OPTIONAL EXTRA: serve with 1 avocado, chopped and dressed with lemon juice (+75 cals per quarter).

...quick **Quorn chilli**

209 CALORIES PER PORTION

Serves 4

Quorn has a quarter of the fat of beef, and it works well in dishes with plenty of heat and spice.

Cooking oil spray
2 medium onions, diced
1 celery stick, finely chopped
2 garlic cloves, crushed
1 tsp chilli powder
½ tsp chilli flakes
Salt and pepper
400g Quorn mince
1 400g tin cherry tomatoes

2 tbsp tomato purée
1 400g tin kidney beans,
  rinsed and drained
200ml veg stock, or boiling
  water and a stock cube
1 tbsp low-fat natural yoghurt
Lime wedges, sweet paprika
  and a generous handful of
  chopped parsley, to serve

Heat oil in a large pan. Gently fry onion, celery and garlic over a medium heat for 3-4 minutes or until softened. Add chilli, season, stir and cook for a further minute. Add Quorn, mix well to combine, then add tomatoes, tomato purée, kidney beans and stock. Cook for 10-15 minutes, and serve with a swirl of yoghurt. Garnish with sweet paprika, chopped parsley and lime wedges.

...low-cal chilli con carne

241 CALORIES PER PORTION

Serves 4

450g lean beef mince
Cooking oil spray
2 onions, diced
2 garlic cloves, crushed
1 red pepper, diced
1 tsp chilli powder (add more or
  less, to taste)
½ tsp crushed chilli flakes
1 tsp ground cumin
1 bay leaf

250g mushrooms, sliced
1 400g tin cherry tomatoes
2 tbsp tomato purée
Pinch of caster sugar
200ml beef stock, or boiling
  water with an Oxo cube
1 400g tin kidney beans, rinsed
  and drained
Salt and pepper

Fry off the beef in a large frying pan until browned and set aside. Heat
oil and gently fry onion, garlic and pepper for 3-4 minutes until softened.
Add spices, bay, mushrooms, tomatoes, tomato purée and sugar and
cook for a further 3-4 minutes. Add browned meat and stock to the pan
and simmer for 15 minutes. Add beans and cook for another 30 minutes –
longer if possible to enrich the chilli. Season and serve.

Traditionally, of course, a chilli tends to demand carbs on
the side. But on a Fast Day, avoid rice, tortillas or jacket
potatoes and serve instead with:

● steamed kale, spinach, broccoli, sugar snaps or finely
sliced cabbage (+25-35 cals per 100g)

● roasted marrow, courgette or red onion wedges (+20
cals per 100g)

SKINNY SPAG BOL

180 CALORIES PER PORTION

Serves 4

A family classic, but here I've lowered the GI count and raised the fibre by bumping up the veg. My father always adds mixed spice to his bolognaise sauce, and I'd recommend its addition for an authentic Italian touch.

Cooking oil spray
400g lean minced beef
1 large onion, diced
1 garlic clove, crushed
1 celery stick, diced
1 red pepper, diced
200g mushrooms, chopped
½ tsp mixed herbs

1 tsp mixed spice
1 400g tin cherry tomatoes
3 tbsp tomato purée
1 courgette, diced
200ml beef stock, or boiling
   water with an Oxo cube
1 tsp Marmite
Salt and pepper

Spray a large pan with a little oil, then fry off the meat until browned and set aside in a separate bowl. This is an important stage as the sugars from the meat will lend your bolognaise colour and flavour. Add onion, celery and pepper to the pan and cook gently for 2-3 minutes until softened. Add mushrooms, herbs, mixed spice, tomatoes and tomato purée and cook for a further 3 minutes. Add browned mince and courgette, together with the stock and Marmite. Cover and simmer, stirring occasionally, for 30 minutes – longer if possible to enrich the sauce. Check seasoning and serve.

Instead of pasta, serve with:

● steamed broccoli and cauliflower florets (+30-35 cals per 100g)

● veg 'noodles' – stir-fried ribbons of courgette, carrot and leek (+35 cals per 100g)

BORLOTTI-BEAN BOLOGNAISE

180 CALORIES PER PORTION

Serves 2

A vegan alternative to the classic spag bol – high in fibre, low in fat and full of good things.

Cooking oil spray
2 garlic cloves, crushed
1 onion, chopped
1 red pepper, diced
100g button mushrooms, sliced
1 tsp mixed herbs

1 400g tin cherry tomatoes
1 tbsp tomato purée
Pinch of caster sugar
1 400g can borlotti beans,
   drained and rinsed
Salt and pepper

Heat oil in a large pan and gently fry the onion, garlic and pepper for 3 minutes until softened. Add mushrooms, herbs, sugar, tomatoes, tomato purée and sugar and cook for a further 3 minutes. Add beans, then cover and simmer for 20-30 minutes until the sauce has reduced. Season and serve.

OPTIONAL EXTRAS: add a handful of chopped black olives (+40 cals) and garnish with torn basil leaves.

FAST FISH PIE

233 CALORIES PER PORTION

Serves 4

Swap dense mash for light-weight filo – you'll get a tasty, filling fish pie that comes in well under the Fast Day calorie count.

Cooking oil spray
1 250g bag spinach leaves
200g half-fat crème fraîche
Handful of fresh dill, chopped
Handful of parsley, chopped
1 tbsp Dijon mustard
1 tsp lemon juice

250g skinless white fish fillet,
  cut into chunks
250g skinless smoked haddock
  fillets, cut into chunks
300g cooked king prawns
Salt and pepper
3-4 sheets filo pastry

Preheat oven to 180°C. Lightly spray an ovenproof dish with oil. Pierce spinach bag and microwave on full power for 90 seconds. Remove from bag and squeeze out as much moisture as possible (press it between kitchen paper), and use the dry spinach to line the ovenproof dish. Mix the crème fraîche with the herbs, mustard, lemon juice, fish and prawns. Season and spoon over the layer of spinach. Spray filo sheets with a little oil, then scrunch them and place on top of the fish mix. Bake for 25-30 minutes until filo is crisp.

FAST DAY TIP: filo pastry generally demands a liberal brushing with melted butter. Here, I've used cooking oil instead to cut down on calories – use sparingly and work fast; filo has a habit of drying out if you hang around.

OPTIONAL EXTRA: add a couple of halved hard-boiled eggs for an extra bump of protein (+40 cals per portion). You can also add chopped watercress to the fish mixture, or a handful of frozen peas.

COQ AU VIN

239 CALORIES PER PORTION

Serves 4

A French institution, made lighter here with the merest hint of oil, just enough pancetta for flavour, and less than half a bottle of white wine. And it still tastes heavenly, promise.

Cooking oil spray
4 large chicken thighs, skinned but on the bone
50g pancetta, diced
2 carrots, peeled and diced
2 onions, diced
2 celery sticks, diced
2 garlic cloves, crushed
2 tbsp plain flour

300ml chicken stock
300ml dry white wine
Handful of tarragon leaves, chopped
Handful of thyme leaves, picked and chopped
1 sprig rosemary
250g button mushrooms, halved
Salt and pepper

Heat a large flameproof casserole dish and spray with oil. Season chicken pieces and brown on all sides until golden. Remove from the pan and set aside. Add pancetta to the pan and fry for 2 minutes until it releases its flavour and is coloured. Add carrots, onion, celery and garlic and cook for 2 minutes. Add flour, stir well and cook for 1 minute, then add wine and stock, scraping the base of the pan to collect the sticky bits. Return chicken to pan, and add the herbs. Cover and simmer on a low heat for 1 hour. Add mushrooms and cook for a further 30 minutes with the lid off. Season and serve.

OPTIONAL EXTRA: instead of button mushrooms, use a mix of shiitake, oyster, chanterelles or ceps.

● goes well with a little gem salad plus Fast Day dressing, P159.

HOT PAPRIKA GOULASH

275 CALORIES PER PORTION

Serves 4

600g braising (or stewing) beef, trimmed of fat and cubed
Cooking oil spray
2 onions, sliced
2 garlic cloves, crushed
1 tbsp paprika
2 tsp Hungarian smoked paprika
400ml beef stock, or boiling water with an Oxo cube
1 400g tin cherry tomatoes
2 tbsp tomato purée
½ tsp caster sugar
2 tsp cider vinegar
2 bay leaves
1 red pepper, deseeded and roughly chopped into chunks
1 yellow pepper, deseeded and roughly chopped into chunks
3 carrots, peeled and cut into chunks
Salt and pepper
2 tbsp low-fat natural yoghurt and chopped parsley to serve

Preheat oven to 180°C. Season the beef with plenty of cracked black pepper. Heat a large flameproof, lidded casserole and spray with cooking oil. Fry off the beef to colour and seal it, remove meat and set aside, then add the onions to the pan. Cook for 5 minutes until onions start to soften, adding a tablespoon of stock if they look like sticking. Then add the garlic and cook for a further minute, stirring well. Return the beef to the pan, add the paprikas, then the stock (or Oxo and boiling water), together with the tomatoes, tomato purée, cider vinegar, sugar and bay leaves. Season and bring to a simmer. Cover and transfer to the oven for 1½ hours, then add peppers and carrots. Stir and return to oven for another hour so the beef is gloriously tender. Serve with a swirl of natural yoghurt and a generous handful of chopped parsley.

● goes well with spiced red cabbage, p131.

SMOKED HADDOCK GRATIN

276 CALORIES PER PORTION

Serves 4

1 250g bag baby spinach leaves
4 smoked haddock portions,
   approx. 150g each
1 tbsp seedy mustard
250g half-fat crème fraîche

50g mature Cheddar, grated
Zest of a lemon
1 beef tomato, sliced
Salt and pepper
Parsley or dill to serve

Preheat oven to 180°C. Pierce spinach bag and microwave on full power for 90 seconds. Remove spinach from bag and squeeze out as much moisture as possible (press it between kitchen paper) before transferring to an ovenproof dish. Combine mustard, crème fraîche, cheese and lemon zest; season carefully (the fish and the cheese will be salty). Place fish over the drained spinach and spoon the crème fraîche mixture on top. Top with tomato slices and bake for 30 minutes. Serve garnished with freshly chopped parsley or dill.

OPTIONAL EXTRA: add 100g cooked peeled prawns beneath the crème fraîche mixture (+89 cals).

TANDOORI CHICKEN WITH MINT DIP AND SAAG ON THE SIDE

279 CALORIES PER PORTION

Serves 4

Ditch the heavy-going sauces and the mound of rice (have spiced spinach instead), and you can grab a curry for under 300 calories.

For the chicken
250g low-fat natural yoghurt
2 tbsp tandoori spice mix
Juice of a lemon
Salt and pepper
8 chicken drumsticks, skinned

For the dip
3 tbsp low-fat natural yoghurt
Handful of fresh mint leaves
1 green chilli, deseeded and
  finely sliced (to taste)
Salt and pepper

For the saag on the side
Cooking oil spray
1 onion, diced
2 garlic cloves, crushed
2cm fresh root ginger, grated
½ tsp ground coriander
½ tsp ground turmeric
½ tsp cayenne pepper
½ tsp garam masala
2 cardamom pods
2 ripe tomatoes, cored and
  diced
500g spinach leaves, chopped
Salt and pepper

Combine yoghurt, spice mix, lemon, salt and pepper in a bowl to make a marinade. Slash the chicken and add to the bowl. Mix well. Cover with clingfilm and chill in the fridge for an hour, or overnight if possible. Preheat oven to 200°C. Place chicken on a wire rack over a roasting tin and bake for 20 minutes (or until it is cooked through), turning after 10 minutes. Meanwhile, for the saag, heat a large pan, spray with oil and fry the onion over a medium heat for 5 minutes. Add garlic and cook for a further 2 minutes. Add ginger, spices and tomato and cook for 2 minutes. Add the spinach in handfuls and cook until it wilts. Remove from heat and season. Combine dip ingredients in a small bowl and serve with the hot drumsticks and a side of the spiced saag.

BASIC BOEUF BOURGUIGNON

294 CALORIES PER PORTION

Serves 4

1 tbsp vegetable oil
600g braising beef, trimmed of
 fat and cut into cubes
250g shallots, peeled (pour
 boiling water over them to
 release the skins)
1 onion, sliced
2 tbsp plain flour
Salt and pepper
500ml red wine

400ml vegetable or chicken
 stock
3 garlic cloves, crushed
1 bouquet garni
1 cinnamon stick
2 large field mushrooms, cut
 into chunks
2 large carrots, peeled and
 roughly chopped
Chopped parsley, to serve

Preheat oven to 160°C. Heat oil in a large, lidded flameproof casserole and sear the beef until lightly browned on all sides. Remove from pan and set aside. Add shallots to the same pan, fry for 3-5 minutes or until nicely browned on all sides. Remove from pan and set aside. Fry off the onion in the same pan, with a tablespoon of stock if it is sticking. Return the beef to the pan and sprinkle in the flour, stirring as you go. Cook for a further 2 minutes, stirring all the time. Season. Gradually add wine and stock, plus garlic, bouquet garni and cinnamon stick. Stir well to incorporate the stickiness at the base of the pan, cover tightly and place in the oven for 2 hours. Add browned shallots, mushrooms and carrots, and return to oven and cook, lid on, for a further 45 minutes. Serve scattered with chopped parsley.

● goes well with steamed green beans. Perhaps add a touch of finely chopped garlic to them for a Gallic flourish.

FAST DAY FISHCAKES WITH THAI SALAD

297 CALORIES PER PORTION

Serves 4

4 boneless, skinless salmon
  fillets
2 tbsp Thai red curry paste
2cm fresh root ginger, peeled
  and grated
1 tsp soy sauce
Handful of coriander
Cooking oil spray
Lime wedges, to serve

For the salad
2 carrots, peeled and ribboned
1 small cucumber, peeled and
  ribboned
100g beansprouts
2 spring onions, finely sliced
1 tbsp lime juice
1 tbsp Thai fish sauce
½ tsp caster sugar
Handful of mint leaves
Handful of coriander

Pulse the fish in a food processor together with the curry paste, ginger, soy and coriander, until you have a rough mince. Shape into 4 patties, each one 1½-2cm thick. Heat a non-stick frying pan, spray with oil and fry the fishcakes for 4 minutes on each side, turning until crisp and cooked through. Prepare the salad by combining the ingredients. Serve alongside the hot fishcakes, with a little more coriander and some lime wedges – and perhaps some chilli dipping sauce on the side, P160 (+19 cals per tbsp).

OPTIONAL EXTRA: add julienned green papaya to the salad (+39 cals per 100g). This salad is also delicious with simple grilled prawns.

SUPER-FAST THAI GREEN CHICKEN CURRY

331 CALORIES PER PORTION

Serves 2

Yes, this is a chicken curry – but for a Fast Day, the meat should play second fiddle to a proper medley of veg. Use whatever you have to hand, and whatever you fancy today: baby 'pea' aubergines, young courgettes, baby sweetcorn, mange touts, broccoli florets, pak choi, thinly sliced peppers, green beans, shiitake or oyster mushrooms, beansprouts, frozen petits pois or spinach… Just don't overcook the veggies – they need to retain a bit of bite.

400ml half-fat coconut milk
1 tbsp Thai green curry paste
100ml chicken stock
1 tbsp lime juice
1 tbsp Thai fish sauce
200g chicken breast, cut into strips

200g vegetables
1 green chilli, finely sliced
Handful of coriander leaves
Lime wedges, to serve

Heat 1 tbsp of coconut milk in a pan, stir in the curry paste and cook for 2 minutes to release the flavour and aroma of the paste. Add the rest of the coconut milk, stock, lime juice and fish sauce. Bring to a low simmer and cook for 10 minutes. Add the chicken strips and vegetables of your choice, and continue to simmer until chicken is cooked through – about 5 minutes. Top with fresh chilli and coriander leaves, and serve with a wedge of lime.

● try this with prawns, tofu or salmon instead of chicken – these will all require slightly less cooking time, around 3-4 minutes.

● goes well with zero-calorie shirataki noodles.

FAST DAY BIRYANI

337 CALORIES PER PORTION

Serves 4

200g basmati rice, rinsed
½ tsp saffron strands
2 cloves, bruised
2 cardamom pods, bruised
400ml cold water
1 tbsp vegetable oil
1 onion, finely sliced

2 garlic cloves, crushed
1 tsp cumin seeds, crushed
1 tsp nigella seeds
400g mini chicken fillets
1 tsp ground cumin
Salt and pepper

Put the rice, saffron, cloves and cardamom in a saucepan with the cold water. Bring to the boil, then reduce heat to low, cover and cook for 10 minutes, or until all the water has been absorbed; once cooked, leave the lid on. Heat the oil in another pan, add sliced onions, garlic, crushed cumin and nigella seeds, and fry until the onions and garlic start to soften – 3-4 minutes. Season the chicken fillets with salt, pepper and ground cumin, then sauté in the same pan for a minute so that the chicken picks up some colour. Cover with a lid and cook for a further 3-4 minutes or until chicken is cooked through. Combine with the cooked rice, check seasoning, and serve.

COTTAGE PIE

340 CALORIES PER PORTION

Serves 2

1 tsp olive oil
300g extra lean minced beef
1 large onion, diced
2 carrots, peeled and diced
2 celery sticks, finely chopped
1 400g tin chopped tomatoes
2 tbsp tomato purée
1 tbsp Worcestershire sauce
1 bay leaf

1 tsp thyme leaves, chopped
300ml boiling water
2 Oxo cubes
500g celeriac, peeled and cubed
100g half-fat crème fraîche
Salt and pepper
1 tsp vegetable oil
2 young leeks, trimmed and
    sliced (pound-coin width)

Preheat oven to 200°C. Heat oil in a large pan and brown minced beef; add diced onions, celery and carrots and cook for 10 minutes until softened. Stir in chopped tomatoes, tomato purée, Worcestershire sauce, bay leaf, thyme, salt and pepper, water and Oxo cubes. Bring to boil, cover and simmer for 30 minutes, stirring occasionally. Boil celeriac until very tender, drain and mash with crème fraîche until smooth. Heat vegetable oil in a pan and gently sauté leeks, then add them to the celeriac mash. Pour beef mixture into a shallow ovenproof dish and top with celeriac mash. Bake for 20-30 minutes, or until the top is golden brown. Serve with plenty of green leafy veg or steamed broccoli.

● swap celeriac mash for a mix of carrot, parsnip or sweet potato or a combination of the three.

● add mushrooms, chopped leeks and lentils to bump up the meat mix – or add a layer of peas.

FAST DAY TIP: make this in individual ramekins to control portion size; it also cooks more quickly and will freeze well in the ramekin.

MOUSSAKA

390 CALORIES PER PORTION

Serves 4

2 tsp olive oil
1 medium onion, sliced
2 red or orange peppers,
  deseeded and sliced
3 garlic cloves, crushed
200g lean minced lamb
100g red lentils
1 tsp dried oregano, or 2 tsp
  fresh oregano
1 tsp allspice
1 500ml carton tomato passata
1 tbsp tomato purée

Pinch of caster sugar
1 aubergine, sliced into 1cm
  rounds
Salt and pepper
4 tomatoes, sliced
25g Parmesan, grated
200g half-fat crème fraîche
1 egg, beaten
Freshly grated nutmeg and an
  extra scatter of Parmesan

Heat 1 tsp oil in a large pan and gently fry the onion and peppers for 5-7 minutes – adding a dash of water if necessary to stop them sticking. Add the garlic and cook for a further minute, then add the lamb, and cook until it starts to brown. Add the lentils, oregano, allspice, passata, tomato purée, sugar and a splash of water. Season and simmer for 15-20 minutes or until the lentils are tender, adding more water if you need to. Heat the grill, place the aubergine and tomato slices on a foil-lined or non-stick baking tray. Brush with remaining teaspoon of olive oil, season, then grill for 4 minutes on each side until slightly blackened. Combine Parmesan, crème fraîche, beaten egg and salt and pepper. Spoon the meat mixture into an ovenproof dish and top with the sliced aubergine and tomato. Add the crème fraîche mix and sprinkle with a grating of nutmeg and a little extra grated Parmesan. Place under a hot grill for 3 minutes until it starts to brown and bubble. Serve with a simple green salad.

CHEAT'S TIP: use frozen sliced peppers and tinned lentils to save on prep time (1 400g tin, drained).

EXPRESS KEDGEREE

397 CALORIES PER PORTION

Serves 4

Cooking oil spray
1 red onion, finely chopped
1 tsp ground coriander
1 tsp curry powder
1 garlic clove, crushed
2 cardamom pods
2cm fresh root ginger, peeled and grated
Pinch of chilli flakes, to taste
A few strands of saffron
Salt and pepper

200g brown rice, rinsed and drained
500ml water
100g frozen petits pois
200g smoked mackerel fillets, flaked
2 hard-boiled eggs, quartered
Snipped chives and lemon wedges, to serve

Heat a large pan, spray with cooking oil and gently fry onion for 3 minutes until softened. Add spices, garlic, cardamom, ginger, chilli flakes, saffron, salt and pepper and fry for a further 2 minutes. Stir in the rice. Cover with water and bring to the boil. Cook on a low heat until rice is almost cooked and the water has been absorbed. Add the peas and cook through – a few minutes. Remove from the heat and carefully add the flaked mackerel and the quartered eggs. Check seasoning and garnish with snipped chives and lemon wedges.

● for a more delicate kedgeree, use smoked trout instead of mackerel fillets.

Lightning quick

Really fast Fast food

There are days when life's a blur. These aren't the leisurely, luxury days when you can spend hours in the company of a recipe, sieving, dicing and marinating, flour up to your elbows and your head in a cook book. These are the real Fast Days. The evenings when you walk through the door, plonk down your bag, pick up a fork. What you want then is speed cooking. With just a little planning, you can eat well – and well within the Fast Diet calorie quota – using ingredients hauled quickly from the cupboard or the fridge.

PRAWN AND ASPARAGUS STIR FRY

105 CALORIES PER PORTION

Serves 2

Once you've assembled your ingredients, the whole cooking process should be done in 6 minutes – which is not much longer that it would take to microwave a ready-meal. And look at the calorie count. Minuscule.

1 tsp vegetable oil
1 onion, sliced
2 garlic cloves, crushed
1 tsp ground ginger
1 red bird's eye chilli, deseeded and finely chopped
4 spring onions, finely sliced on the diagonal
1 stalk lemongrass, bruised
2 lime leaves

3 tbsp Thai fish sauce
2 tbsp boiling water
½ tsp palm sugar
12 raw king prawns
300g asparagus, halved lengthways and cut into 3cm pieces
Coriander leaves, Thai basil leaves, lime wedges, to serve

Heat the oil in a wok, and stir fry onion, garlic, ginger and chilli until softened. Add spring onions, cook for a further minute, then add the lemongrass, lime leaves, fish sauce, water and sugar. Stir, then add the prawns and asparagus. Cook on high for 3 minutes or until the prawns are pink and the asparagus is *al dente*. Remove lemongrass. Serve with fresh coriander leaves, Thai basil and a wedge of lime.

OPTIONAL EXTRAS: add 100g of halved baby sweetcorn (+25 cals) and sugar snaps (+35 cals) along with the asparagus for bulk and vibrant colour.

FAST DAY CHICKEN
6 SPEEDY WAYS...

...with gremolata and dark leaves

140 CALORIES PER PORTION

Serves 4

Gremolata is a vivid green Italian sauce made from finely chopped garlic, lemon zest and masses of parsley, traditionally served with osso bucco, but a great way to pimp any plain grilled or seared meat or fish.

For the gremolata
Generous handful of flat-leaf
  parsley, finely chopped
1 tbsp extra-virgin olive oil
Zest of a lemon
1 tbsp lemon juice
1 tsp fresh oregano, finely
  chopped
1 tsp fresh thyme, finely
  chopped

2 garlic cloves, very finely
  chopped
Salt and pepper

4 chicken thighs, boneless and
  skinless
2 tsp olive oil
Salt and pepper
Dark salad leaves or blanched
  green beans, to serve

In a small bowl, combine the parsley, most of the olive oil, lemon zest, lemon juice, oregano, thyme, garlic, salt and pepper. Stir well and set aside. Slash the meat several times, drizzle with remaining olive oil and season well, then place on a hot griddle pan. Cook on a medium heat until golden and sticky, then turn and continue until meat is cooked through (approx. 5 minutes each side). Serve drizzled with 1 tbsp gremolata and a side of dark salad leaves such as watercress, rocket, lambs lettuce, purslane, sorrel or baby spinach.

...with piri piri sauce

163 CALORIES PER PORTION

Serves 4

1 tsp olive oil
4 boneless and skinless chicken
   thighs, trimmed of excess fat,
   scored

For the piri piri sauce
1 small red onion, roughly
   chopped
2 cloves of garlic, peeled

1-2 bird's-eye chillies (to taste)
1 tbsp smoked paprika
Juice of ½ lemon
2 tbsp white wine vinegar
Salt and pepper
2 tsp fresh thyme leaves
2 red or orange peppers,
   deseeded and cut into chunks

Preheat oven to 200°C. Drizzle the chicken with olive oil and season well, then place in a hot griddle pan. Cook on a medium heat until just golden, then turn and continue to brown for 3-4 minutes. For the piri piri sauce, place onion, garlic, chillies, paprika, lemon juice, vinegar, salt and pepper and thyme in a small food processor and whizz to a paste. In a small roasting pan, combine chopped peppers, browned chicken pieces and piri piri sauce, coating everything well. Bake until chicken is thoroughly cooked – about 15-20 minutes – turning halfway through cooking, .

● for extra stickiness, this sauce can be rubbed into a whole chicken and roasted.

FAST DAY TIP: if you have the calorie allowance for a more substantial meal, increase the portion size to two thighs each. This will raise the calorie count to 303 per person, still well within the Fast Day ration.

...with peppers and capers

179 CALORIES PER PORTION

Serves 4

1 tsp olive oil
4 boneless and skinless chicken
thighs, trimmed of excess fat,
scored
Salt and pepper
2 red peppers, deseeded and
finely sliced

2 garlic cloves, sliced
1 sprig rosemary
150ml water
1 chicken stock cube
2 tbsp capers, rinsed
200g baby spinach
Zest of a lemon, to serve

Drizzle the chicken with olive oil and season well, then place in a hot griddle pan. Cook on a medium heat until just golden, then turn and continue to brown for 3-4 minutes. Remove chicken from pan and set aside. Add peppers, garlic and rosemary to the pan and fry for 3-4 minutes. Return chicken to the pan, add stock cube and water, and stir well to combine. Simmer for 20 minutes or until sauce is reduced and the chicken is cooked through. Add capers and spinach, and stir on the heat for a further 2 minutes. Serve with a sprinkle of lemon zest.

...with Dijon marinade

210 CALORIES PER PORTION

Serves 2

One of my favourite answers to the perennial 'what's for supper?' question – this is fast, tasty and pleasingly low in fat.

300g mini chicken breast fillets
Salt and pepper
1 tbsp Dijon mustard

2 tbsp low-fat natural yoghurt
2 tsp herbes de Provence

Combine all ingredients in a bowl, season and set aside. Griddle chicken pieces for 3-4 minutes on each side or until they are cooked through and nicely striped. Serve with a squeeze of lemon and a simple green salad.

FAST DAY TIP: marinate the chicken in a plastic bag in the morning or the previous night and refrigerate to infuse it with maximum flavour.

...with masala and raita

221 CALORIES PER PORTION

Serves 4

4 skinless chicken thighs,
  scored
200g low-fat natural yoghurt
2 tbsp masala paste
2 garlic cloves, crushed
Salt and pepper
Handful of coriander,
  chopped
Zest and juice of a lime

For the raita
200g low-fat natural yoghurt
1 cucumber, peeled, halved,
  deseeded and sliced
Fresh mint leaves
Squeeze of lemon
Salt and pepper

Preheat oven to 200°C. Combine the chicken with the yoghurt, masala paste, garlic, half the chopped coriander, lime juice and zest in a bowl. Set aside in the fridge to marinate for 30 minutes or more if you have time. Place chicken in a small roasting pan and bake for 20 minutes or until it is cooked through. Combine raita ingredients and serve alongside chicken, topped with more lime zest and a scatter of coriander leaves.

FAST DAY TIP: you may want to cook the chicken with its skin on to retain juice and flavour, but don't eat it. I prefer to remove most of the skin before marinating to get the flavour well absorbed into the meat.

FAST DAY TIP: the masala yoghurt marinade also works well with a whole chicken; slash the meat and cover with the marinade. Massage into the meat and marinate overnight. Cook in preheated oven at 200°C until juices run clear (1-1½ hours).

...Chinese spice

273 CALORIES PER PORTION

Serves 2

300g mini chicken breast fillets
1 tbsp soy sauce
1 tbsp mirin
1 garlic clove, crushed
½ tsp Chinese five-spice powder

2 tsp honey
1 tsp sesame oil
2 star anise
1 red chilli, finely sliced, to serve

Combine ingredients in a bowl and set aside in the fridge (you can do this the night before if you get the chance – a longer marinating time will allow the flavours to develop more fully, but if you're strapped for time, it's fine to cook immediately). Griddle chicken pieces for 3-4 minutes on each side or until they are cooked through and nicely striped. Serve with plenty of black pepper and a scatter of finely sliced red chilli.

● goes well with steamed pak choi (+12 cals per 100g).

NO-FUSS FISH WITH CHILLI DRESSING

175 CALORIES PER PORTION

Serves 2

2 fresh white fish fillets –
   haddock, cod, plaice, pollack
   (approx. 200g per fillet)
Salt and pepper

For the dressing
1 red chilli, deseeded and very
   finely chopped

Pinch of caster sugar
2 tbsp Thai fish sauce
2 tbsp lemon juice
2 tbsp chopped parsley
Snipped chives

Mix dressing ingredients in a bowl. Steam or bake seasoned fish fillets until cooked through and opaque. Spoon dressing over fish and serve with a simple green salad or plenty of steamed broccoli.

● **CHEAT'S TIP**: place fish fillet in a microwaveable bowl, add slices of lemon and cover with clingfilm. Punch a hole in the film and cook on full power until opaque – about 3 minutes.

● goes well with Asian sesame salad, P137.

WARM CHICKEN LIVER SALAD

184 CALORIES PER PORTION

Serves 4

Chicken livers may not (yet) top your shopping list, but when properly cooked – seared on the outside, rose-pink within – they can be delectable. Better yet, they're high in protein and folate, and full of iron. You'll need dense, flavourful leaves here to balance the robust meatiness of the livers.

Cooking oil spray
250g chicken livers
200g fine green beans
1 large bag of salad leaves –
  include interesting leaves such
  as pea shoots and raddichio

4 tbsp Fast Day dressing, P159
1 tbsp sherry vinegar
Squeeze of lemon
Salt and pepper

Heat a small frying pan and spray with oil. Season livers and cook for 5-6 minutes (or more if the livers are thicker), turning once, aiming for a crisp exterior with a little pinkness within. Blanch green beans in boiling water for 2-3 minutes so they are tender but *al dente*. Place leaves and blanched beans in a bowl and dress with Fast Day dressing. Add cooked livers and check seasoning. Deglaze the cooking pan with vinegar and a squeeze of lemon, then drizzle over salad.

FAST DAY TIP: this works well with baby herbs for extra layers of flavour.

OPTIONAL EXTRA: scatter a handful of toasted chopped hazelnuts (+60 cals per 10g) for a little crunch and extra protein.

FIVE-MINUTE ROAST BEEF SALAD

248 CALORIES PER PORTION

Serves 2

This is grab-a-bag cooking. And none the worse for it.

240g pre-prepared carrot, cauliflower and broccoli florets in a bag
100g cooked roast beef – slices from yesterday's roast or shop bought, the thinner and rarer the better

Salt and pepper
Generous handful of watercress and rocket leaves

2 tbsp Fast Day dressing, P159
2 tbsp shaved Parmesan, to serve

Microwave the veg in their bag on full power for 3-4 minutes. Drizzle the Fast Day dressing over the warm vegetables. Add watercress and rocket, and top with strips of rare roast beef and shavings of fresh Parmesan. Season well with cracked black pepper and serve.

CHICKPEA CURRY IN A HURRY

249 CALORIES PER PORTION

Serves 2

Five minutes. One store cupboard. Two forks. Done.

Cooking oil spray
1 onion, diced
2 garlic cloves, crushed
3 tsp curry powder
¼ tsp dried chilli flakes
200ml boiling water
1 vegetable stock cube

2 tbsp tomato purée
1 400g tin chickpeas, rinsed and
  drained
Salt and pepper
1 tbsp low-fat natural yoghurt,
  to serve

Heat a pan and spray with oil. Gently fry the onion and garlic until softened. Add curry powder and chilli flakes and cook for a further 2 minutes. Add boiling water, stock cube, tomato purée and chickpeas. Simmer until chickpeas are heated through and the sauce thickened. Season and serve with a swirl of natural yoghurt, and perhaps a salad of thinly sliced cucumber.

OPTIONAL EXTRAS: add a handful of spinach leaves or 10 cherry tomatoes (+35 cals) for the last 2 minutes of cooking.

FAST DAY TIP: to make a curry with more complexity, add a cinnamon stick, 3 curry leaves, a clove, 1 tsp nigella seeds, a halved chilli and a couple of cardamom pods to the pan with the frying onion; add 2 tbsp ground almonds (+70 cals) for a thicker curry sauce.

GARAM MASALA TUNA STEAK

324 CALORIES PER PORTION

Serves 1

Tuna is a sturdy fighter of a fish that can well take the impact of these heavyweight spices. My preference is to eat it rare, but go with your instincts here.

1 tsp fennel seeds
2 tsp garam masala
Salt and pepper
½ tbsp fresh root ginger, grated
Handful of fresh coriander,
 finely chopped

3-4 mint leaves, finely chopped
1 tuna steak, about 2cm thick
 (approx. 200g)
½ tbsp vegetable oil
Lemon juice, to serve

Crush fennel seeds, garam masala and salt and pepper with a pestle. Add ginger, coriander and mint leaves and pound to a paste. Rub on both sides of tuna steak. Refrigerate for an hour or more. Heat oil and griddle tuna on high until cooked to your liking. Serve with a squeeze of lemon.

● goes well with fine green beans (+25 cals per 100g).

BAKED FALAFEL WITH TWO DIPPING SAUCES

380 CALORIES PER PORTION

Serves 2

You can make your own falafel, or course, but it's a faff and the packet versions can be just as good. Bake, don't fry, and you achieve a decent Fast Day supper for relatively few calories. Add veggies and leaves of your choice – my favourites are included here.

8 ready-made falafel balls
2 wholewheat pitta breads
½ romaine lettuce, shredded
1 carrot, peeled and grated
2 ripe tomatoes, diced
½ red onion, finely sliced
Sliced green jalapeño peppers
   from a jar (optional)

Handful of baby spinach
   leaves
Coriander leaves

Hummus, let down with a little
   water to make a runnier sauce
Chilli dipping sauce, P160

Preheat oven to 200°C. Place falafel in a small foil-lined roasting tray and bake for 10-12 minutes, turning halfway through cooking. Warm the pittas, slit lengthways and fill with lettuce, carrot, diced tomato, red onion, spinach leaves and coriander. Add falafel and drizzle each portion with 1 tbsp hummus and 1 tbsp chilli dipping sauce. Serve with a napkin (it's a messy business).

QUICK ROAST PORK LOIN WITH BROCCOLI AND CAULIFLOWER CHEESE

386 CALORIES PER PORTION

Serves 4

I like the ease and relative fatlessness of a good pork tenderloin. Have it with cheesy veg for a great supper on a cold day – or try it with any of the chicken accompaniments from P48-54.

1 pork tenderloin fillet (approx. 450g)
1 tsp olive oil
2 tsp fennel seeds, crushed
Salt and pepper

150g cauliflower florets
150g broccoli florets
175g pre-prepared cheese sauce
50g mature Cheddar, grated

Preheat oven to 200°C. Rub pork loin with a little olive oil, then season and roll in crushed fennel seeds. Place in a small roasting pan and bake for 20-25 minutes, depending on the thickness of the fillet, until cooked through. Cover with foil during cooking time if the meat is colouring too much. Leave to rest. Meanwhile, boil, steam or microwave cauliflower and broccoli. Drain well and place in a small ovenproof dish. Heat cheese sauce and pour over drained vegetables – ensure that they are as dry as possible to prevent weeping. Top with Cheddar and place in hot oven for 5 minutes to melt cheese. Cut the rested pork into medallions, pour the pan juices on top and serve with a goey spoonful of cheesy veg.

FAST DAY TIP: use mature rather than mild Cheddar to maximise flavour and keep calories in check. Or use feta for its strong flavour and relatively low calorie count.

PEPPERED PORK WITH SUMMER SLAW

467 CALORIES PER PORTION

Serves 2

2 pork loin steaks
1 tsp olive oil
Cracked black pepper
Sea salt

For the slaw
1 green apple, skin on,
   grated
¼ white cabbage, shredded
2 tbsp chopped chives
75g half-fat crème fraîche
1 tsp honey
Juice of a lemon

Preheat oven to 200°C. Rub the pork with olive oil, season with cracked black pepper and sea salt, and sear in a griddle pan on all sides. Cover with foil. Turn the oven off and transfer griddle pan to the cooling oven for 8-10 minutes, or until the pork is cooked through. Remove from oven and rest for 5 minutes. Combine apple slaw ingredients, mix well and serve alongside pork.

OPTIONAL EXTRAS: add 1 tbsp sultanas (+48 cals) and 1 tbsp walnuts (+50 cals) to the slaw for extra sweetness and crunch.

...OR WITH WARM WINTER SLAW

493 CALORIES PER PORTION

Serves 2

2 pork loin steaks
1 tsp olive oil
¼ tsp chilli flakes
2 tsp cracked black pepper
½ tsp sea salt

For the slaw
¼ white cabbage, finely
   shredded
¼ red cabbage, finely shredded
1 carrot, peeled and julienned
2 spring onions, finely sliced

1 tbsp raisins
Handful of fresh coriander

For the dressing
1 tbsp sherry vinegar
1 tbsp olive oil
½ tbsp walnut oil
1 tsp runny honey
¼ tsp chilli flakes
1 garlic clove, crushed
Salt and pepper

Preheat oven to 200°C. Rub the pork with olive oil. Combine pepper, salt and chilli flakes in a small bowl and sprinkle over meat. Heat an ovenproof griddle pan and sear the pork for two minutes on each side. Cover with foil. Turn the oven off and transfer griddle pan to the cooling oven for 8-10 minutes or until cooked through. Remove from oven and rest for 5 minutes. Meanwhile, prepare the winter slaw. Combine dressing ingredients in a small saucepan and gently warm through. Pour over salad ingredients and toss well. Check seasoning. Serve in a plentiful mound alongside the rested pork.

FAST DAY OMELETTES

plain

150-190 CALORIES, DEPENDING ON SIZE OF EGGS

Serves 1

There are few square meals that can beat an omelette on a Fast Day. Swift. Tasty. Filling. And all done in one lone pan.

2 medium eggs
Cooking oil spray
Salt and pepper

Beat the eggs with a fork until bubbly. Add salt and plenty of pepper, and cook gently in a small frying pan until the omelette is set to your liking.

or try an omelette with:

- 1 tsp curry spices added to the egg mix **+0 cals**

- 1 tbsp finely chopped pimentos **+10**

- 50g cooked prawns and 1 tbsp chopped coriander **+45**

- 1 tbsp ricotta and a handful of spinach leaves **+46**

- 100g lightly steamed or microwaved mushrooms (drained) and a scatter of freshly chopped parsley **+55**

- 1 tbsp cooked crab meat and 1 tbsp shaved parmesan **+55**

- 1 chopped spring onion and ¼ tsp chilli flakes, lightly fried, topped with 10g crumbled goat's cheese and a handful of chopped parsley **+66**

- steamed asparagus topped with 2 torn slices of Parma ham **+75**

- 50g smoked trout, 1 finely sliced spring onion, 1 tsp chopped fresh dill and 1 tbsp low-fat cream cheese **+85**

- 50g low-fat mozzarella, 4 sliced tinned artichoke hearts and a chopped ripe tomato **+85**

- 50g feta cheese, 3 chopped black olives and a scatter of fresh sage **+120**

- 50g torn smoked salmon and chopped chives topped with a swirl of low-fat crème fraîche just before serving, perhaps with 1 tsp rinsed capers **+160**

- 50g crumbled chèvre and 1 tbsp DIY oven-dried tomatoes, P161 **+175**

- 50g grated mature Cheddar and 50g frozen petits pois **+275**

STRAIGHT TO THE PLATE...

Not recipes so much as great flavour combinations, grabbed from your fridge and kitchen cupboards, on days when you don't want to think too hard about food (or indeed precise calorie counts... All the below are Fast Day friendly suggestions). Just add the simple Fast Day dressing from page 159 where desired or required.

- smoked mackerel fillet, watercress, plum tomatoes
- tuna, cannellini beans, red onion
- roast beetroot, grilled halloumi, rocket
- avocado, prawns, low-fat crème fraîche
- mozzarella, avocado, ripe tomato
- Parma ham, melon, strawberries
- blanched French beans, cooked king prawns, feta
- hummus, raw veggies, jalapeños
- white cabbage, red onion, hardboiled egg
- smoked chicken, romaine lettuce, cashews
- pilchards, cherry tomatoes, steamed broccoli florets
- beef carpaccio, toasted pine nuts, rocket, Parmesan
- chicken tikka pieces, beef tomato, cucumber raita
- lean roast beef, horseradish crème fraîche, little gem

Warming and wonderful

Comfort food for hungry days

If you've been on the Fast Diet for some time, you may well have had your fill of salad leaves. So, what about the days when you're in need of something warm, something substantial, the culinary equivalent of a cuddle? That's where these stews, curries and casseroles come in. You'll know them all, but here, well-loved recipes have been relieved of superfluous calories to make them ideal for a Fast Day. Many are freezer friendly, so make them in bulk and tuck in.

SHOOTS AND LEAVES RED CURRY

128 CALORIES PER PORTION

Serves 4

1 tbsp vegetable oil
1 large onion, cut into wedges
1 red pepper, deseeded and
  sliced
2 garlic cloves, chopped
2 tbsp Thai red curry paste
300ml vegetable stock
2 tbsp Thai fish sauce
1 tsp soft brown sugar

1 200g tin bamboo shoots,
  drained
200g beansprouts
1 220g tin water chestnuts,
  drained and sliced
2 tbsp coriander, chopped
200g young spinach leaves
25g peanuts, chopped
Handful of basil leaves

Heat oil in a wok or large frying pan, add onion, pepper and garlic and fry on a medium heat for 5 minutes or until softened. Add curry paste and cook for a further 2 minutes. Add stock, fish sauce and sugar. Bring to the boil, stir, lower heat and simmer for 15 minutes. Add bamboo shoots, bean sprouts, chestnuts and coriander, and cook uncovered for a further 15 minutes, adding the spinach towards the end of the cooking time. Serve with a scatter of chopped peanuts and basil leaves.

● goes well with shirataki noodles or Asian sesame
salad, P137 (+133 cals per portion).

MONKFISH CURRY

137 CALORIES PER PORTION

Serves 4

For the paste
Cooking oil spray
1 onion, chopped
4 garlic cloves
1 tsp nigella seeds
1 red chilli, deseeded
2 tsp ground coriander
2 tsp ground cumin
1 tsp chilli powder
1 tsp garam masala
½ tsp ground turmeric
2 tbsp water

For the curry
1 400g tin cherry tomatoes
250ml water
2 tbsp low-fat natural yoghurt
1 tsp mango chutney
Juice of half a lemon
3-4 monkfish tails, cut into
    chunks (approx. 600g)
100g baby spinach leaves
Salt and pepper

2 tbsp low-fat natural yoghurt
    and coriander leaves, to serve

To make the curry paste, heat a large frying pan, spray with oil and fry the onion and garlic until soft; add the nigella seeds and cook for a further 2 minutes. Place this cooked onion mix in a blender and add all the other paste ingredients. Blitz. Put this paste in the pan and fry for 2-3 minutes before adding water and chopped tomatoes. Cook until sauce is slightly reduced, then add mango chutney and lemon juice. Add monkfish and simmer until cooked through, throwing in spinach leaves for the last 2 minutes of cooking. Remove from heat, check seasoning and swirl in yoghurt and fresh coriander.

● goes well with nut-brown rice: for 4 people, boil 200g brown basmati; dry-fry 75g mixed chopped nuts and stir into the cooked rice. Top with a scant grating of nutmeg and serve (+299 cals per portion). If you're up against your quota for the day, just have plain brown rice.

THREE TAGINES...

There's plenty of warmth and tenderness here. Unleash the fragrant aromas with a flourish of the lid as you serve.

...chicken tagine with preserved lemons and saffron

162 CALORIES PER PORTION

Serves 4

Cooking oil spray
4 chicken thighs, skinned
  but on the bone
2 onions, finely chopped
1 celery stick, finely chopped
3 garlic cloves, crushed
4 ripe tomatoes, deseeded and
  sliced
350ml chicken stock
½ tsp saffron threads
½ tsp ground turmeric
½ tsp ground cumin

½ tsp paprika
1 tsp ground coriander
1 tsp runny honey
3cm fresh root ginger, grated
1 cinnamon stick
2 small preserved lemons, finely
  chopped
1 tsp harissa paste
Salt and pepper
Squeeze of lemon, handful of
  coriander leaves and
  pomegranate seeds, to serve

Heat a little oil in a tagine or large flameproof casserole, add chicken pieces and brown all over. Add onions, celery and garlic and sweat on a low heat for 10 minutes, stirring occasionally. Add tomatoes, stock, saffron, turmeric, cumin, paprika, coriander, honey, ginger, cinnamon stick, preserved lemons and harissa. Stir, replace lid and simmer on a low heat for 1½ hours. Season well. Just before serving, shred chicken off the bone and return to pot. Serve garnished with a squeeze of lemon, and plenty of chopped coriander and pomegranate seeds.

...vegetable tagine with herbed couscous

311 CALORIES PER PORTION

Serves 4

For the tagine
1 tbsp olive oil
2 onions, thinly sliced
2 tsp ground cumin
2 tsp ground coriander
1 tsp ground ginger
2 garlic cloves, crushed
2 tbsp harissa paste
2 carrots, peeled and cut into chunks
2 parsnips, approx. 500g, peeled and cut into chunks
1 small butternut squash, approx. 500g, peeled, deseeded and cut into chunks

500ml vegetable stock, or boiling water and a vegetable stock cube
75g dried apricots, chopped
1 tbsp lemon juice
1 400g tin chickpeas, rinsed and drained

For the couscous
300g couscous
1 tbsp pine nuts, toasted
Handful of flat-leaf parsley, chopped
Handful of coriander, chopped
Lemon zest, to serve

Heat oil in a tagine or large flame-proof casserole, add onion and cook for 5 minutes until softened. Add the spices and garlic and cook for a further minute. Add harissa and vegetables, season, and stir well. Pour over the stock, add the apricots and lemon juice and simmer gently for 30 minutes. Add chickpeas and continue cooking for 10 minutes more. Prepare couscous as per packet instructions, leaving to stand for 10 minutes, and then fluffing up with a fork and adding pine nuts and chopped herbs. Serve tagine and couscous in a deep bowl, scattered with coriander and lemon zest.

...Moroccan spiced lamb

349 CALORIES PER PORTION

Serves 4

Cooking oil spray
600g lean lamb leg steaks,
    trimmed of fat and cut into
    3cm cubes
2 onions, peeled and sliced
2 garlic cloves, crushed
Salt and pepper
2 tsp ground cumin
2 tsp ground coriander
½ tsp ground cinnamon
1 tsp chilli powder
1 400g tin cherry tomatoes
400ml boiling water

1 lamb stock cube
2 tbsp runny honey
1 400g tin chickpeas, rinsed
    and drained
1 bay leaf
1 medium sweet potato,
    approx. 200g, peeled
    and cut into 3cm chunks
50g stoned prunes, halved
Generous handful of flat-leaf
    parsley and lemon zest, to
    serve

Preheat oven to 180°C. Season lamb chunks. Heat a large flameproof casserole with a little cooking oil spray and fry off the lamb, onions and garlic for 2-3 minutes or until lightly coloured. Add the spices, stir and cook for a further 2 minutes. Add tomatoes, boiling water, crumbled stock cube, honey, chickpeas and bay. Stir well and bring to a simmer on the hob. Cover with a tight-fitting lid and transfer to oven. Cook for 1 hour, then add sweet potato chunks and prunes, return to oven and cook for a further 45 minutes. Serve sprinkled with parsley and lemon zest.

● goes well with saffron and shallot sauce: mix 4 tbsp low-fat natural yoghurt with a finely chopped shallot and a few saffron strands. Season and serve on the side (+25 cals per tbsp).

NEAPOLITAN CIANFOTTA

179 CALORIES PER PORTION

Serves 4

This is a loose, family-style recipe for a delicious summer vegetable stew; use what you have and what you like. 'Cianfotta' means tasty and colourful, so keep it light and bright, without too many starchy vegetables. If you like capers, add a teaspoon or two along with the stock for a salty kick.

2 tbsp olive oil
1 onion, finely diced
1 celery stick, finely chopped
1 carrot, peeled and finely diced
3 garlic cloves, crushed
1 fennel bulb, trimmed and cut into 8 wedges
Handful of fresh marjoram or oregano, roughly chopped
1 bay leaf
1 small aubergine, cut into 2cm cubes

4 courgettes, sliced into 2cm rounds
400ml hot vegetable stock
200g cherry tomatoes, halved
200g sugar snap peas
200g mange touts
100g frozen petits pois
4 courgette flowers (if available)
Salt and pepper
Pecorino cheese, to serve

Preheat the oven to 180°C. Heat oil in a large flameproof casserole and gently fry onion until softened. Add celery, garlic, carrot, fennel, bay and marjoram or oregano, cover and sweat for a further 5 minutes. Then add aubergine and courgettes, season, stir, cover and transfer to hot oven for 30 minutes, stirring occasionally to release any stickiness from the pan base. Remove from oven, add vegetable stock and bring to a simmer on the hob. Add cherry tomatoes, sugar snaps, mange touts and petits pois. Adjust seasoning, bring back to a simmer for 3-4 minutes or until the vegetables are just cooked. Serve in deep soup bowls, with a decorative shaving of pecorino (+25 cals per tbsp).

ONE-POT BEAN FEAST

207 CALORIES PER PORTION

Serves 4

Beans are a great source of low-fat, high-fibre protein. Play around with different types for a change of texture, taste and colour. You can buy tins of three bean salad to get a good mix in a single tin.

1 tbsp olive oil
1 large red onion, chopped
2 garlic cloves, crushed
2 carrots, peeled and chopped
2 celery sticks, chopped
1 tbsp fresh thyme, or 1 tsp
   dried thyme
2 400g tins mixed beans
   (haricot, cannellini, kidney,
   pinto, flageolet, adzuki, black
   beans), rinsed and drained

1 400g tin cherry tomatoes
1 tbsp red wine vinegar
1 tbsp runny honey
1 tbsp Dijon mustard
Salt and pepper
1 sprig rosemary
Generous handful of parsley,
   chopped
250ml water
Juice of a lime

Heat olive oil in a large pan and fry red onion and garlic until soft. Add carrots, celery and thyme and cook for a further 5 minutes. Add beans, tomatoes, vinegar, honey, mustard, salt, pepper, rosemary, half of the parsley, and water. Stir, season and bring to a simmer over a low heat and cook, loosely covered, for 2 hours, stirring every half-hour. Remove from heat and add lime juice and the rest of the parsley. Serve with a lemon-dressed leaf salad and plenty of black pepper.

FIRE AND SPICE VEGGIE CASSEROLE

247 CALORIES PER PORTION

Serves 4

1 tsp cumin seeds
1 tsp coriander seeds
1 tsp black mustard seeds
2 tbsp olive oil
3 onions, sliced
3 carrots, peeled and roughly
   chopped
2 leeks, trimmed and sliced
2 garlic cloves, crushed
25g fresh root ginger, peeled
   and finely chopped

1 red chilli, deseeded and finely
   chopped (to taste)
1 tsp chilli powder
¼ tsp ground turmeric
200g split red lentils
450g button mushrooms, halved
750ml boiling water
1 vegetable stock cube
Handful of coriander, chopped
Salt and pepper

Crush seeds with a pestle and mortar. Heat oil in a large flameproof casserole, add onions, carrots and leeks, and fry for 5 minutes. Add garlic, ginger, chilli and chilli powder, turmeric and crushed spices and fry for a further 2 minutes. Stir in lentils and mushrooms, add boiling water and the stock cube. Season, stir, cover and simmer on a low heat for 45 minutes to 1 hour. Stir in coriander before serving.

● goes well with tabbouleh, P133 (+123 cals).

CHICKEN CASSOULET

318 CALORIES PER PORTION

Serves 4

Cassoulet is hearty, rustic and full of beans. It usually contains plenty of fat – sausage, lardons, duck confit, pork skin and the rest – but here, I've slimmed it down so that it fits snugly into a Fast Day. A little chorizo, though not French (*sacré bleu!*), will add depth. It's the slow cooking that lends the required unctuousness, so prep in advance and give it some time to become.

1 tbsp olive oil
2 onions, peeled and sliced
2 celery sticks, chopped
50g chorizo sausage, chopped
2 tbsp tomato purée
8 garlic cloves, unpeeled and
   left whole
2 bay leaves
100ml white wine
100ml boiling water
Juice of half a lemon

3 carrots, peeled and sliced into
   1cm rounds
1 400g tin cherry tomatoes
Salt and pepper
4 chicken thighs, skinned but on
   the bone
1 bouquet garni
1 400g tin cannellini or
   haricot beans
Handful of fresh parsley, finely
   chopped, to serve

Preheat oven to 180°C. Heat oil in a large ovenproof pan, and cook onions and celery over a low heat for 2-3 minutes. When softened, add chorizo and fry for a further minute or until it has released its colour and flavour. Add tomato purée, garlic cloves and bay, stir and cook for a further 5 minutes. Add wine, water and lemon juice, then simmer for 3 minutes to reduce a little. Add carrots and tomatoes and season. Bring back to a simmer, then add chicken pieces, bouquet garni and beans. Stir to coat well in the sauce and transfer to oven for 1-1½ hours until chicken is cooked, tender and falling off the bone. Just before serving, remove the bouquet garni, then mash some of the soft, sweet garlic cloves into the beans and sauce. Scatter with parsley and serve.

ITALIAN RABBIT STEW

328 CALORIES PER PORTION

Serves 4

Rabbit was once a regular on the nation's dinner tables; having fallen out of favour for decades, it's now firmly back on the menu. And there are very good reasons to try it: rabbit can generally be locally sourced (ask your butcher), it's a comparatively sustainable source of meat, relatively low in fat and satisfyingly cheap.

2 tbsp olive oil
1 rabbit, cut into portions
1 onion, finely sliced
4 spring onions, chopped
2 celery sticks, chopped
2 carrots, peeled and chopped
4 garlic cloves, crushed
1 tsp capers
½ tsp fresh thyme
2 sprigs rosemary
1 tsp dried oregano
2 bay leaves
200ml white wine
150g chestnut mushrooms, roughly chopped
25g porcini mushrooms, rehydrated in boiling water for 15 minutes and drained
3 ripe tomatoes, chopped
Juice and zest of a lemon
Salt and pepper

Preheat oven to 180°C. Heat olive oil in a large ovenproof casserole, season rabbit and fry to brown on all sides. Add all other ingredients except the lemon zest, stir to combine any stickiness from the pan base and bring to a simmer. Cover with a tight-fitting lid and transfer to oven. Cook for 1 hour, or until rabbit is tender, and the sauce has become flavourful and rich. Serve garnished with the zest of the lemon and cracked black pepper.

● if rabbit is hard to come by, this dish can be made equally well with chicken.

● goes well with baked fennel, P134 (+123 cals), cannellini bean mash, P138 (+183 cals).

CHICKEN PROVENÇAL

348 CALORIES PER PORTION

Serves 4

Another French classic – just slim-line.

8 skinless and boneless chicken
  thighs, cut in half
Cooking oil spray
2 medium onions, sliced
2 garlic cloves, crushed
1 400g tin cherry tomatoes
2 tbsp tomato purée
150ml chicken stock – or
  boiling water and a
  chicken stock cube

2 tsp herbes de Provence
100ml red wine
1 red pepper, deseeded and cut
  into chunks
1 yellow pepper, deseeded and
  cut into chunks
2 medium courgettes, cut into
  2cm rounds
Salt and pepper

Trim any excess fat off the chicken and season well. Spray a large non-stick frying pan with oil and fry chicken pieces over medium heat for 5-6 minutes, or until lightly coloured. Add onions, garlic, tomatoes, tomato purée, stock, herbs and wine. Stir well. Bring to a simmer and cook for 10 minutes, stirring occasionally. Add peppers and courgettes, bring back to a simmer, then cover and cook for 20-25 minutes, or until chicken is cooked through. Season and serve.

● this sauce is delicious with king prawns too; use 400g raw prawns instead of the chicken and cook for 15 minutes in total.

● goes well with spring greens with mustard seeds, P126 (+27 cals per portion).

KASHMIRI CHICKEN AND YOGHURT CURRY

368 CALORIES PER PORTION

Serves 4

1 tsp olive oil
8 skinless and boneless chicken
  thighs, cut into thick strips
1 large onion, thinly sliced
5cm fresh root ginger, peeled
  and grated
2 garlic cloves, crushed
1 green chilli, finely chopped

Handful of coriander, the roots
  and stems finely chopped
1 tsp ground coriander
1 tsp ground turmeric
2 cardamom pods
100ml chicken stock
200ml low-fat natural yoghurt
Salt and pepper
Coriander leaves, to serve

Heat oil in a large pan and brown the chicken strips for 2-3 minutes. Remove from pan and set aside on kitchen paper. Add onion, ginger, garlic, chilli and chopped coriander roots and cook for 10 minutes. Add the spices and cook for a further 5 minutes, stirring well. Return browned chicken to pan, add stock and yoghurt (it may separate a little as it cooks), season, stir and simmer gently for 30 minutes. Serve sprinkled with fresh coriander leaves.

● goes well with saag on the side, P129 (+68 cals per portion).

CHICKEN CURRY WITH LEMONGRASS AND GINGER

394 CALORIES PER PORTION

Serves 4

8 skinless and boneless chicken
  thighs
2 tbsp curry powder
Salt and pepper
1 tbsp olive oil
4 shallots, sliced
1 red chilli, finely chopped
1 garlic clove, crushed
1 lemongrass stalk, bruised

5cm fresh root ginger, peeled
  and sliced
2 tbsp Thai fish sauce
1 tbsp lemon juice
250ml chicken stock
250ml half-fat coconut milk
200g mange touts
Fresh coriander leaves, to serve

Toss chicken thighs in curry powder, and season with salt and pepper. Heat oil in a large heavy-bottomed pan. Fry shallots, chilli and garlic for 2 minutes or until softened. Add chicken and cook to seal and lightly brown. Add lemongrass, ginger, fish sauce, lemon juice, stock and coconut milk. Bring to boil, cover and simmer for 25 minutes, then add the mange touts. Simmer for a further minute or two, ensuring chicken is cooked through, and serve topped with coriander leaves.

● goes well with shirataki noodles.

BEEF AND BEER CASSEROLE

398 CALORIES PER PORTION

Serves 4

Cooking oil spray
2 onions, roughly chopped
2 tbsp plain flour
Salt and pepper
2 tsp mixed herbs
1kg lean braising beef, trimmed
    of fat and cut into 3cm cubes
1 bay leaf
500ml dark ale

250ml beef stock, or boiling
    water and an Oxo cube
1 tbsp tomato purée
3 carrots, peeled and sliced into
    2cm rounds
500g button mushrooms, halved
    if large

Preheat oven to 180°C. Fry onions in a little cooking oil spray for 4-5 minutes. Dust the beef in the flour seasoned with salt, pepper and the herbs, then place it in a large casserole dish with the cooked onions, bay, stock, ale and tomato purée. Cover and cook in the oven for 2-2½ hours, adding the carrots and mushrooms for the last hour, then serve.

● goes well with spiced red cabbage, P131 (+ 79 cals per portion), or any of the mash alternatives, P138.

BOSTON BEANS AND HAM

401 CALORIES PER PORTION

Serves 4

You'll get an unctuous, sticky plate of good food from this recipe.
Go slow and savour.

1 850g smoked gammon joint
Cooking oil spray
1 onion, finely chopped
1 garlic clove, crushed
1 tbsp tomato purée
2 tbsp maple syrup
2 tsp English mustard powder
¼ tsp chilli flakes

1 tsp paprika
½ tsp ground cinnamon
2 400g cans haricot beans,
  rinsed and drained
300ml chicken or vegetable
  stock
Black pepper

Preheat the oven to 180°C. Soak the gammon in cold water for 15
minutes to release some of its saltiness. Dry well. Either leave rind and
string on, or remove; you can also cut it in half to aid cooking (trimmed
weight should be approx. 700g). Spray a flame-proof casserole with oil
and fry the gammon over a medium heat until brown on all sides. Remove
from pan and set aside on kitchen paper. Add the onion to the casserole
and fry for 2 minutes, stirring well to release meat flavours from the
pan base. Add garlic, tomato purée, maple syrup, mustard powder, chilli
flakes, paprika and cinnamon. Stir well and cook for a further minute, then
add the beans and stock and heat through. Add the browned gammon,
cover with a tight-fitting lid and transfer to the oven for 45-50 minutes,
removing the lid for the final 10 minutes to reduce the sauce. Season well
with black pepper, check for saltiness, then remove the gammon. Serve
it sliced on top of the beans with some steamed, iron-rich greens to cut
through the richness of the stew.

BEEF DAUBE WITH PEPPERED GREENS

429 CALORIES PER PORTION

Serves 4

The slow cooking here intensifies the flavour without requiring too much fat. I like the idea of dark veg with this – an earthy tangle of steamed kale, purple sprouting broccoli or grilled radicchio would be perfect. The orange zest is an essential component – and do be generous with the pepper.

2 tbsp plain flour
Salt and pepper
1kg lean braising beef, trimmed
  of fat and cut into 3cm cubes
1 large red onion, sliced
4 garlic cloves, crushed
1 400g tin cherry tomatoes
2 carrots, peeled and cut into
  chunks
3 sprigs of thyme
1 bay leaf

Juice of an orange
Peel of half an orange
350ml white wine
400ml beef stock, or boiling
  water and an Oxo cube
4 anchovy fillets, finely chopped
50g black olives
500g curly kale or spring greens
A grating of orange zest and
  cracked black pepper to serve

Preheat oven to 170°C. Toss beef cubes in well-seasoned flour and place in a large casserole along with all the other ingredients except the greens and the orange zest. Bring to a simmer on the hob, stir, cover with a tight-fitting lid and then transfer to oven. Cook until the beef is tender and the sauce thickened – 2-3 hours. Serve with steamed greens, a grating of orange zest and a final flourish of cracked black pepper.

Fast-600

Filling Fast Day meals for men

As a historical rule, men don't tend to be wild about dieting. They don't like the faff – all that counting and measuring, the eating from dolly plates and saying no to the roast potatoes. But the Fast Diet seems to be different: men have been adopting it in droves. They appear to like the clarity of the 600-calorie, twice-a-week rule. On a Fast Day, many men choose to eat nothing at all (staying hydrated, of course) until the evening, when they'll sit down to a decent meal. That's where this chapter comes in. Man food. Under 600 cals. Done.

SIMPLE SEARED SIRLOIN, AND 5 QUICK ACCOMPANIMENTS...

183 CALORIES PER PORTION FOR A PLAIN STEAK

Serves 1

1 200g sirloin steak, trimmed of
  visible white fat

A little olive oil
Salt and pepper

Heat a griddle pan until searingly hot. Rub steak with a little olive oil, season well and sear for 2-3 minutes on each side or until cooked to your liking. Rest and prepare with one of the following:

...rocket and watercress with horseradish cream

+80 CALORIES PER PORTION

2 tbsp low-fat crème fraîche
1 tsp horseradish sauce
Juice of half a lemon

Snipped chives
Handful each of rocket and
  watercress

Combine ingredients and serve alongside the steak and a generous mass of rocket and watercress leaves. If you have calories to spare, add a scant crumble of blue cheese (+45 cals per tbsp).

...pepper sauce

+104 CALORIES PER PORTION

Cooking oil spray
2 small shallots, finely chopped
100ml chicken stock
1 tbsp low-fat garlic soft cheese

1 tsbp low-fat crème fraîche
1 tsp coarsely crushed
    peppercorns

After removing the steak and setting aside to rest, spray the griddle pan
with oil and fry shallots until softened. Lower the heat and add the stock,
soft cheese, crème fraîche and crushed peppercorns and stir together
well with a spatula. Simmer for 2 minutes until the sauce is slightly
thickened, then drizzle on rested steak. Curly kale would be good on the
side.

...chilli dipping sauce and pak choi

+109 CALORIES PER PORTION

1 red chilli, deseeded and very
    finely chopped
1 garlic clove, crushed
1 tsp caster sugar
1 tbsp Thai fish sauce

1 tbsp lime juice
1 tbsp chopped mint
150g pak choi, sliced into
    strips

Mix sauce ingredients in a bowl. Steam pak choi for 3 minutes and drain
well. Slice steak thinly, and serve on top of the hot pak choi, drizzled with
dipping sauce.

...herb dressing

+130 CALORIES PER PORTION

Handful of tarragon leaves,
  chopped
Handful of basil leaves, torn
1 tbsp olive oil

½ tbsp lemon juice
½ tbsp white wine vinegar
½ tsp caster sugar

Combine ingredients well and pour over the steak and your chosen veg.
Fine green beans or lightly steamed asparagus would be ideal.

...busted tomatoes and olives

+140 CALORIES PER PORTION

1 vine (approx. 8-10) cherry
  tomatoes
½ tbsp olive oil

Pinch of chilli flakes
Salt and pepper
4 black olives, halved and pitted

Preheat the oven to 200°C. Place ingredients in a small ovenproof dish
and bake for 15-20 minutes. Serve alongside the steak, spooning over the
tomato juices.

GARLIC AND PARSLEY PRAWNS

215 CALORIES PER PORTION

Serves 2

Prawns are a Fast Dieter's faithful friend – under 60 calories per 100g, easy to haul from the freezer, and a bolt of protein with no carbs and barely any fat.

24 raw king prawns, peeled,
  tails intact (approx. 200g)
3 small garlic cloves, crushed
1 tbsp olive oil
1 tbsp lemon juice

1 tbsp flat-leaf parsley, finely
  chopped
Salt and cracked black pepper
Lemon wedges, to serve

Combine all the ingredients in a bowl and rest in the fridge to allow flavours to develop. Heat a griddle pan to medium-hot and cook the prawns for 2-3 minutes, turning once – they should be pink but still juicy. Serve with lemon wedges and a substantial bowl of lemon-dressed herb salad.

FAST DAY TIP: griddling seals in flavour while allowing any excess cooking fat to run off along the ridges of the pan. Look for a heavy griddle pan with well-spaced ridges; when cooking, don't be tempted to move the fish or meat around too much, even if it appears to be sticking. Have faith: once cooked, it will unstick itself.

● goes well with chunky cumin coleslaw, P130 (+74 cals).

TEN-MINUTE KING PRAWN CURRY

222 CALORIES PER PORTION

Serves 2

Prawns are also one of the speediest fridge-to-plate options around. This really does take ten minutes end to end – if you eat it slowly and with relish, it should take longer to consume than to cook.

2 tbsp medium or hot curry paste (for example Patak's Tikka Masala paste)
2 tbsp cold water
1 red onion, finely sliced
1 red pepper, deseeded and sliced
1 red chilli, deseeded and finely chopped

1 tbsp mango chutney
3 large ripe tomatoes, cored and roughly chopped
150ml half-fat coconut milk
200g cooked or raw king prawns
100g baby spinach leaves
Fresh coriander leaves and lime juice, to serve

Heat a large pan and add curry paste, water, onion, pepper and chilli and cook for 4 minutes, until softened, stirring well. Add chutney, tomatoes and coconut milk and simmer for 3 minutes. Add prawns and spinach, cook until the prawns are pink and the spinach has just wilted – about 3 minutes. Serve with a squeeze of lime and coriander leaves.

OPTIONAL EXTRAS: a shop-bought low-calorie naan bread would add 120 calories.

CHILLI BEEF STIR FRY

230 CALORIES PER PORTION

Serves 4

1 tsp olive oil
4 spring onions, sliced on the
  diagonal
400g lean minced beef
3cm fresh root ginger, grated
3 garlic cloves, crushed
1 tsp Chinese five-spice powder
½ tsp chilli powder

250ml beef stock, or boiling
  water and an Oxo cube
3 tbsp soy sauce
150g mange touts
150g sugar snap peas
1 red chilli, deseeded and finely
  sliced, to serve

Heat oil in a large wok and stir fry spring onions for 1 minute. Then add
the beef and cook for a further 5-6 minutes or until browned. Add the
ginger, garlic, five-spice and chilli powder and fry for a few minutes more.
Add the stock and soy sauce, bring to the boil, stirring occasionally, and
simmer for 5 minutes. Add sugar snaps and mange touts and cook until
the vegetables are just done. Serve topped with red chilli slices.

OPTIONAL EXTRAS: add 100g chopped oyster or
shiitake mushrooms along with the mange touts to bulk
out the dish at negligible calorie cost.

● goes well with fresh egg noodles, if your calorie
count allows (+130 calories per 100g).

QUICK-FIRE BURGERS WITH HOT TOMATO SAUCE

234 CALORIES PER PORTION

Serves 4

I love these fiery burgers. By all means, use leftover lamb – but make sure that you're using the least fatty meat: the fat in lamb can quickly bust your calorie count.

For the sauce
250ml tomato passata
1 tbsp tomato purée
1 red chilli, halved and
   deseeded to taste
1 tsp dried oregano
½ tsp caster sugar

For the burgers
Cooking oil spray
400g lean cooked lamb, minced
1 small onion, finely chopped
2 garlic cloves, crushed
1 tbsp harissa paste
30g breadcrumbs
Salt and pepper
2 eggs, beaten
4 tbsp low-fat plain yoghurt and
   chopped coriander, to serve

Simmer sauce ingredients in a small saucepan for 20 minutes and set aside. Mix burger ingredients in a large bowl. Divide into 8 patties. Spray a large frying pan with oil and fry the burgers on a medium heat until browned. Lower the heat and cook for a further 5-10 minutes until cooked, turning once. Serve with the hot sauce on the side, plus a cooling tablespoon of low-fat natural yoghurt, chopped coriander and a lemon-dressed side salad.

OPTIONAL EXTRAS: add fresh mint, dried rosemary and thyme, or chopped capers to the burger mix.

● goes well with courgette and almond salad, P141 (+253 cals).

LAMB STEAKS WITH MUSHY PEAS

263 CALORIES PER PORTION

Serves 4

1 tsp olive oil
2 tbsp balsamic vinegar
2 tsp thyme leaves
Salt and pepper
4 lamb steaks, approx. 100g
  each, trimmed of excess fat

400g frozen peas
30g butter
Handful of mint leaves, chopped
Squeeze of lemon

Combine olive oil, balsamic vinegar, thyme and salt and pepper in a bowl or plastic bag. Add lamb steaks and coat well, then leave for up to a day in the fridge to marinate. Heat a griddle pan until very hot, and sear the marinated lamb for 1-2 minutes on each side, or until done to your liking. Meanwhile, cook the peas, strain, and then blend them with butter, mint, lemon and sea salt. Serve with the rested lamb.

EASY LAMB KEBABS

267 CALORIES PER PORTION

Serves 4, making 8 kebabs

For the marinade
2 tsp ground cumin
2 tsp ground coriander
½ tsp chilli flakes
1 tsp fennel seeds
1 tbsp fresh thyme leaves
Zest and juice of a lemon
1 garlic clove, crushed
1 tbsp olive oil
Salt and pepper

For the kebabs
700g lean lamb, cubed and
   trimmed of excess fat
2 red onions, cut into wedges
   (keep the root intact)
2 courgettes, cut into 3cm
   rounds
2 yellow peppers, deseeded and
   cut into chunks
2 red peppers, deseeded and
   cut into chunks
1 lemon, cut into 8 wedges

Combine marinade ingredients in a bowl or plastic bag. Add the lamb and leave to marinate in the fridge for at least an hour, or preferably overnight. Prepare the kebabs on metal skewers, alternating meat and veggies and ending with a lemon wedge. Brush with any remaining marinade. Cook under a hot grill for 6-8 minutes, turning occasionally and spooning over any excess marinade. These are great barbecued, of course, or cooked on a hot griddle pan.

● goes well with chunky cumin coleslaw, P130 (+74 cals).

OPTIONAL EXTRA: add firm mushrooms or aubergine cubes to boost your veggie intake.

HUEVOS RANCHEROS

283 CALORIES PER PORTION

Serves 1

Add a little Mexican twist to suppertime (or to breakfast, for that matter, if you're looking for something substantial). Eggs are a prime Fast Day food, and this way of serving them is a welcome break from the usual suspects.

1 tsp olive oil	1 tsp balsamic vinegar
2 spring onions, finely chopped	2 eggs
1 red pepper, sliced	Handful of flat-leaf parsley,
¼ tsp chilli flakes	roughly chopped
1 200g tin chopped tomatoes	Salt and pepper

Heat oil in a small frying pan and gently fry spring onion, red pepper and chilli flakes for 3 minutes. Add tomatoes and vinegar. Season, stir and simmer for 5 minutes. Make two dips in the sauce and crack an egg into each. Continue cooking until the whites have begun to set, then cover and cook until they are completely set, but the yolks are still runny. Sprinkle with parsley and serve.

OPTIONAL EXTRA: serve with avocado (+150 cals per half), chilli sauce (25 cals per tbsp) and a wholemeal tortilla (approx. 90 calories) if you want the full enchilada. The total calorie count per portion would then be 548.

TURKEY KOFTE WITH TZATZIKI AND WARM PITTA

310 CALORIES PER PORTION

Serves 4

Using turkey mince rather than the traditional lamb really lowers the calorie count of these tasty kofte.

For the kofte
500g lean turkey mince
3 garlic cloves, crushed
1 tsp ground cumin
1 tsp ground coriander
½ tsp chilli flakes
½ tsp allspice
Zest of half a lemon
2 tbsp fresh mint, chopped
2 tbsp flat-leaf parsley, chopped
Salt and pepper
Cooking oil spray

For the tzatziki
100g low-fat natural yoghurt
1 garlic clove, crushed
½ small cucumber, peeled, deseeded and diced
Coriander leaves, chopped
Mint leaves, chopped
Squeeze of lemon
Salt and pepper

4 wholemeal pitta breads
2 tsp cumin seeds, dry-fried in a small frying pan

Combine kofte ingredients in a large bowl until evenly mixed, then shape around 8 metal or pre-soaked wooden skewers. Chill for half an hour, spray with a little oil, then place on a lightly oiled, foil-lined baking sheet and grill on a medium-high heat for 10-12 minutes, turning once. Combine the tzatziki ingredients in a small bowl. Place kofte in warmed pitta breads, drizzle with tzatziki and scatter with the cumin seeds.

FAST DAY TIP: if you have the kofte and tzatziki without the pitta, the calorie count dives to 173 per portion. Kofte freeze well so it's worth making in double quantities.

MADRAS BEEF WITH A TOMATO AND RED ONION SALAD

319 CALORIES PER PORTION

Serves 4

1 tbsp vegetable oil
1 onion, sliced
2 garlic cloves, crushed
2 green peppers, deseeded and
  sliced
3 cardamom pods, bruised
1 cinnamon stick
4 red chillies, 2 deseeded and
  finely chopped, 2 split
2 tsp Madras curry powder
1 400g tin cherry tomatoes
1 tbsp tomato purée

800g stewing or braising steak,
  trimmed of fat and cut into
  3cm cubes
½ tsp caster sugar
Salt and pepper
450ml beef stock, or boiling
  water and an Oxo cube
10 okra, trimmed and sliced

For the salad
2 red onions, thinly sliced
2 beef tomatoes, thinly sliced
Coriander, to serve

Preheat oven to 170°C. Heat oil in a flameproof casserole and fry onion, garlic, green peppers, cardamom, cinnamon stick and chopped chilli for 5-7 minutes. Add curry powder, stir, cook for a further minute or two, then add tomatoes and tomato purée. Cook over a medium heat for 5 minutes, stirring all the time. Add beef, halved chillies, sugar, salt and pepper. Stir well to ensure the beef gets a good coating, and cook for a further 2 minutes. Add stock, bring to a simmer, cover and transfer to the oven. Cook for 1½ hours or until beef is tender, adding the okra 20 minutes before the end of cooking time. Serve with a salad of red onion and tomatoes, with torn coriander and plenty of black pepper.

OPTIONAL EXTRA: if you want rice with your curry, include 50g brown basmati per person. It's a decent Fast Day source of slow-release carbohydrates, and is nutty and nutrient-rich (+77 cals).

PANKO 'FRIED' CHICKEN

335 CALORIES PER PORTION

Serves 4

Not fried, of course. But the panko – a Japanese-style breadcrumb that doesn't absorb as much fat as traditional crumbs – delivers a crispy-crunchy coating which is just as good to eat.

250ml buttermilk
Salt and pepper
1 tsp ground ginger
1 tsp ground turmeric
2 tsp ground coriander
2 tsp paprika

4 chicken drumsticks
4 chicken thighs
Cooking oil spray
100g panko
Lemon wedges, to serve

Combine buttermilk, salt and pepper, ginger, turmeric, half the coriander and half the paprika in a large bowl. Add chicken and toss. Leave to marinate in the fridge for 3 hours, or overnight if possible. Preheat oven to 190°C. Put panko in a bowl and season with remaining coriander, paprika, salt and pepper. Coat each chicken piece in seasoned panko. Place on baking tray lined with non-stick foil, or sprayed with a little cooking oil. Bake for 35-40 minutes or until golden brown and cooked through, turning once if necessary. Serve with lemon wedges and a simple green salad.

● goes well with big baked beans, P149 (+265 cals).

CHEAT'S TIP: if buttermilk is hard to find, substitute with 200ml low-fat plain yoghurt mixed with 50ml semi-skimmed milk.

SEA BASS WITH TOMATO, CHORIZO AND BUTTER BEANS

385 CALORIES PER PORTION

Serves 2

This is one of my all-time great standby suppers, particularly if I'm having friends over to eat. It looks great, tastes utterly delicious and is surprisingly fool-proof.

2 sea bass fillets, approx. 200g
each
30g chorizo sausage, roughly
chopped
10 cherry tomatoes, halved
1 garlic clove, crushed
1 tsp dried parsley

1 400g tin butter beans
Salt and pepper
1 250g bag baby spinach
Squeeze of lemon
Cooking oil spray
Fresh parsley, chopped, and
lemon wedges, to serve

Season fillets and score skin to prevent it curling during cooking. Fry chorizo in a dry pan until it releases its oil, flavour and colour. Add tomatoes, garlic and parsley and cook for 2 minutes, until tomatoes soften. Add butter beans and simmer for 2 minutes so they are heated through. Add spinach and lemon juice for the final minute of cooking, then remove from the pan and set aside. Spray a little cooking oil in the same pan and when hot, sear the sea bass skin side down for 3 minutes or until crisp. Flip it over and cook on the other side for 2 minutes. Place on a mound of the warm butter bean mixture and serve with fresh parsley and lemon wedges.

OPTIONAL EXTRA: add 1 tsp of fennel seeds along with the tomatoes and parsley. Or 6 black olives, halved and pitted, for extra depth (+30 cals).

● try sea bream or red mullet fillets as an alternative to sea bass.

VENISON SAUSAGES WITH CANNELLINI BEAN MASH

417 CALORIES PER PORTION

Serves 2

4 venison sausages
2 red onions, each cut into 8 wedges
1 leek, trimmed and cut into 4cm chunks
2 peppers, deseeded and sliced
1 tsp olive oil
Salt and pepper

For the cannellini bean mash
1 400g tin cannellini beans, rinsed and drained
2 tbsp semi-skimmed milk
1 vegetable or chicken stock cube
1 tbsp olive oil

Preheat oven to 190°C. Place vegetables in a shallow ovenproof dish, season, drizzle with oil, cover loosely with foil and bake for 10 minutes. Stir well and lay the sausages on top. Bake under the foil for a further 30 minutes; halfway through, turn the sausages and remove the foil for the final 15 minutes of cooking time. Heat the cannellini mash ingredients and purée with a hand-blender, or mash well with a fork. If too thick, add a dash more milk. Serve alongside sticky sausages and veg.

FAST DAY TIP: venison has a similar nutritional profile to beef but is lower in fat.

OPTIONAL EXTRA: bump up the veggies at negligible calorie cost – perhaps adding fennel wedges or chunks of aubergine. Add a halved red chilli if you want heat.

LAMB IN A PAN

501 CALORIES PER PORTION

Serves 2

What you're really after on a Fast Day is a good whack of flavour. That's what this is all about: the capers and anchovies are a savoury, punchy foil for the lamb. Better yet, the whole meal (including pan-fried chicory) can be on your plate in under 10 minutes.

1 tsp vegetable oil
400g lamb neck fillets,
   approx. 100g each,
   trimmed of excess fat
Salt and pepper

For the dressing
1 tbsp white wine vinegar
½ tsp Dijon mustard
Handful of fresh parsley,
   chopped
4 anchovy fillets, finely chopped
1 tbsp capers, drained and
   finely chopped

Heat a heavy griddle pan. Slice the lamb fillets in half lengthways, rub with a little oil, season and sauté in a hot pan for 4-5 minutes, or more if you prefer it well done. Set aside to rest. Combine dressing ingredients and drizzle over the rested lamb. Serve with your choice of vegetables.

● goes well with pan-fried chicory. Quarter a head of chicory, season and sear in the lamb pan for 2-3 minutes on each side. Add a squeeze of lemon, plenty of black pepper and sea salt and serve alongside lamb, drizzled with dressing (+25 cals per 100g).

MAN FOOD FOR A FAST DAY

Breakfast

If in doubt, eat an egg. A two-egg chilli and spring onion omelette has 180 calories; scrambled eggs with 80g smoked salmon has 300. If you need carbs to start to the day, go for porridge – perhaps with chopped pear and cinnamon (286 calories).

Supper

Max out the veg and minimise the carbs. You need protein too; white fish, shellfish and chicken are best. Add flavour rather than calories with lemon, cumin, chilli, lime, ginger, onion... You can have curry, but if you're short of calories, go for fish or prawns instead of meat. Dahl is an ideal choice, see P147.

Takeaways

Sashimi boxes are great for a hit of protein (avoid sushi rice). Soup is good too – but go for the clear, veg-laden broths, not the heavier, meaty, cheesy alternatives. Pret's soups can weigh in at 230 calories. At Eat, try Chicken Pho (96) or Ginger Beef Noodle (111).

Snacks

Not really part of the plan. But if you must, have a handful of almonds, or strawberries, carrots and hummus, or an apple. Include the calorie count in your quota.

Drinking

Stay hydrated. Alcohol is 'empty' calories (a 550ml beer racks up 250). If you must, vodka has the fewest calories; soda and lemon juice are the best mixers; orange juice doubles the calorie count of a vodka shot.

Simple sides

Ideal alone, or to partner a supper of chicken or fish

Plenty of people simply eat grilled fish or chicken on a
Fast Day. Here's how to pep up the plate with easy,
healthy sides and salads. You may, of course, choose
to make these dishes the main event; many are full of
protein and need no further fuss.

SPRING GREENS WITH MUSTARD SEEDS

27 CALORIES PER PORTION

Serves 4 as a side dish

1 tbsp mustard seeds
1 tsp olive oil
1 small onion, finely sliced
1 garlic clove, crushed

1 tbsp fresh root ginger, grated
500g spring cabbage, shredded
2 tbsp water

Dry-fry the mustard seeds until they start to pop. Add the oil, then sauté the onion, garlic and ginger until golden. Tip in the shredded cabbage and stir to coat in the spices, add water and then cook for 5 minutes until tender. Season and serve.

CAULIFLOWER 'COUSCOUS'

36 CALORIES PER PORTION

Serves 4 as a side dish

1 large cauliflower, divided into florets

4 tbsp water
Salt and pepper

Place cauliflower in a food processor and pulse until it resembles breadcrumbs. Bring water to a simmer in a large frying pan and add cauliflower crumbs. Steam gently for 3-4 minutes, season and serve.

OPTIONAL EXTRAS: this works with any number of additions. Try adding 1 tsp chopped rosemary or thyme, 2 finely sliced spring onions and 2 tsp lemon zest during the cooking time. Or add 1 tbsp each of finely chopped celery, raisins (+33 cals) and chopped apple (+15) once cooked. Walnuts (+50), pine nuts (+58), orange zest, dried cranberries (+26) and pomegranate seeds (+9) are good additions too – or a simple handful of chopped coriander for colour and flavour.

● goes well with any tagine, P78-81.

SAAG ON THE SIDE

68 CALORIES PER PORTION

Serves 4 as a side dish

Cooking oil spray
1 onion, chopped
4 garlic cloves, finely chopped
2 tsp fresh root ginger, grated
½ tsp ground coriander
½ tsp ground turmeric
½ tsp cayenne pepper

½ tsp garam masala
2 cardamom pods, bruised
500g spinach leaves, washed
    and roughly chopped
100g low-fat natural yoghurt
Squeeze of lemon
Salt and pepper

Heat a large, deep pan and spray with oil. Sauté onion until softened –
about 5 minutes, then add garlic, ginger and spices and cook for a further
2-3 minutes. Add spinach in handfuls, allowing it to wilt down before
adding another handful. Add a dash of water if necessary, and continue
cooking for about 5 minutes, stirring gently. Remove from heat, season
and stir in yoghurt and a squeeze of lemon.

OPTIONAL EXTRA: add a handful of chopped
tomatoes along with the first handful of spinach at
negligible calorie cost.

● goes well with Kashmiri chicken and yoghurt curry,
P91.

CHUNKY CUMIN COLESLAW

74 CALORIES PER PORTION

Serves 4 as a side dish

½ white cabbage, roughly
   shredded
2 carrots, peeled and grated
1 apple, peeled and grated
2 tsp cumin seeds, dry-fried
   in a small frying pan

¼ tsp ground cumin
2 tbsp low-fat natural yoghurt
2 tsp lemon juice
1 tbsp sultanas
Salt and pepper

Combine all ingredients and serve.

OPTIONAL EXTRA: include shredded celeriac or
fennel, or a handful of walnuts (+50 cals) for added
crunch and protein.

● goes well with easy lamb kebabs, P111.

SPICED RED CABBAGE WITH APPLES

79 CALORIES PER PORTION

Serves 6 as a side dish

Cooking oil spray
1 onion, finely diced
2 apples, peeled and cubed
1 medium red cabbage,
   quartered and finely sliced
3 tbsp red wine vinegar
1 bay leaf
1 cinnamon stick

½ tsp ground ginger
½ tsp ground coriander
1 clove
1 cardamom pod
250ml tart apple juice
1 tbsp runny honey
Salt and pepper

Heat a spray of oil in a pan and cook onion until softened. Add apples and cook for 3 minutes, stirring gently. Add cabbage, vinegar, bay, spices, apple juice and honey. Stir, cover and simmer on a low heat for 25 minutes or until cabbage is tender. Season and serve.

- goes well with hot paprika goulash, P31.

- this is even better the next day, and it freezes well.

CELERIAC REMOULADE

92 CALORIES PER PORTION

Serves 4 as a side dish

400g celeriac, peeled

For the dressing
2 tbsp lemon juice

2 tbsp mayonnaise
2 tbsp low-fat plain yoghurt
2 tbsp Dijon mustard
Salt and pepper

Use a food processor or a mandolin to julienne the celeriac into fine matchsticks. Do not grate as it will become too mushy. Toss in the combined dressing ingredients and serve.

OPTIONAL EXTRAS: thinly sliced fennel and celery can be added to the celeriac. Swap the lemon juice for orange juice and add grated carrot as an alternative. Or add an aniseed twist of finely chopped tarragon.

● goes well with smoked mackerel or smoked trout.

TABBOULEH

123 CALORIES PER PORTION

Serves 4 as a side dish

Tabbouleh is a parsley salad, not a bulgar salad; herbs should predominate. As an alternative to bulgar, you could use buckwheat (it is also lower GI).

75g bulgar wheat
1 tsp ground allspice
1 tsp ground cinnamon
1 tsp ground coriander
4 ripe tomatoes, cored and
  chopped
4 spring onions, finely sliced
Juice of 2 lemons

½ large bunch of flat-leaf
  parsley, finely chopped
½ large bunch of fresh mint,
  finely chopped
2 tbsp olive oil
2 tbsp pomegranate seeds
Salt and pepper

Soak the bulgar wheat and spices in almost-boiling water and set aside until softened – about 20 minutes. Fluff up with a fork, then add tomatoes, spring onions and lemon juice. Stir well, add the herbs, pomegranate seeds and olive oil, season and serve.

● if you prefer the tomatoes skinned, immerse them in boiling water for 2-3 minutes and then peel.

BAKED FENNEL WITH PARMESAN AND THYME

123 CALORIES PER PORTION

Serves 2 as a side dish

2 fennel bulbs, trimmed and
  quartered
1 tbsp olive oil
1 tbsp lemon juice

Salt and pepper
30g Parmesan, grated
1 tsp dried thyme, or 1 tbsp
  fresh thyme leaves

Preheat oven to 200°C. Place fennel quarters in a small roasting tin, coat with olive oil and lemon, then season and scatter with the Parmesan and thyme. Cover with foil and bake for 30 minutes until soft.

● goes well with Dijon chicken, P52.

● try this with leeks or chicory, or a mix of all three.

ASIAN SESAME SALAD

133 CALORIES PER PORTION

Serves 2 as a side dish

1 pak choi, sliced into ribbons
Chinese leaves (or Savoy
  cabbage), torn
Handful of beansprouts
Handful of mange touts, sliced
  on diagonal
Handful of watercress
1 carrot, peeled and grated
1 spring onion, sliced on the
  diagonal
Handful of coriander, chopped

For the dressing
1 tsp palm sugar
1 tsp toasted sesame oil
1 tsp soy sauce
½ tbsp Thai fish sauce
Juice of a lime

1 red chilli, finely sliced
  (optional), 10 cashews,
  roughly chopped, and 3 tsp
  sesame seeds, toasted, to
  serve

Assemble salad ingredients, toss with the combined dressing ingredients, and serve topped with cashews, sesame seeds and fresh chilli, if desired.

● goes well with shoots and leaves red curry, P74, or no-fuss fish, P55.

INSTEAD OF MASHED POTATO...

...cauliflower mash

142 CALORIES PER PORTION

Serves 2 as a side dish

1 tbsp olive oil
1 small onion, finely chopped
1 garlic clove, crushed
1 leeks, finely sliced
½ tsp ground turmeric
Salt and pepper

1 small cauliflower, divided into
   florets
50ml vegetable stock, or boiling
   water with half a vegetable
   stock cube
Squeeze of lemon

In a large pan, heat oil and gently fry onion, garlic and leek until softened. Add turmeric, season and cook for as further minute. Add cauliflower and stir well to coat with the spiced onion mix. Add stock, cover and cook gently for 10 minutes. Purée with a hand-held blender, or mash well. Add lemon juice and serve.

...cannellini bean mash

183 CALORIES PER PORTION

Serves 2 as a side dish

1 400g tin cannellini beans,
   rinsed and drained
2 tbsp semi-skimmed milk
1 vegetable or chicken stock
   cube

1 tbsp olive oil
Salt and pepper

Heat ingredients, then purée with a hand-blender or mash well. Return briefly to heat if you like your mash piping hot. Season with plenty of cracked black pepper and serve.

OPTIONAL EXTRA: add chilli flakes, chopped fresh herbs (sage would be good) and a squeeze of lime to the bean mash for extra zing.

FAST DAY TIP: this is very good served cold as a dip for raw veggies; loosen with a little low-fat yoghurt and garnish with parsley, a squeeze of lemon and paprika.

...sweet potato and carrot mash

183 CALORIES PER PORTION

Serves 2 as a side dish

300g carrots, peeled and chopped
300g sweet potatoes, peeled and chopped
2 garlic cloves, crushed

1 tsp cumin seeds, dry-fried in a small frying pan
15g butter
Salt and pepper
2-3 tbsp semi-skimmed milk (optional)

Place the carrots, sweet potatoes and garlic in a large pan of salted water, bring to the boil, then cook until tender – 12-15 minutes. Drain, then add roasted cumin seeds, butter and seasoning. Roughly mash, adding a dash of milk if you prefer a looser consistency, then serve.

FAST DAY TIP: if you can't bear to go without mashed potato, cut the calories by using crème fraîche rather than butter. Or mix with sliced steamed leeks, or add a handful of watercress leaves after mashing, which will wilt prettily in the heat.

THREE WARM SALADS...

...spiced brown lentils with mint

171 CALORIES PER PORTION

Serves 2 as a side dish

200g brown lentils, rinsed
1 bay leaf
Cooking oil spray
1 red onion, finely chopped
1 garlic clove, crushed
½ tsp ground cumin
½ tsp paprika
2 cardamom pods

For the dressing
Generous handful of fresh mint
  leaves, chopped
1 tbsp olive oil
1 tbsp red wine vinegar
Salt and pepper

2 spring onions, finely sliced,
  to garnish

Place lentils in a saucepan with the bay leaf, cover with water and simmer for 15-20 minutes or until tender. Spray a small frying pan with oil and sauté the onion, garlic and spices for 3 minutes until the onion starts to soften. Remove the cardamom pods. In a small bowl, combine dressing ingredients and whisk well. Drain lentils, removing the bay leaf, then combine with onion mix and drizzle with the mint vinaigrette. Serve warm, topped with spring onion.

...yellow courgette and almond

253 CALORIES PER PORTION

Serves 2 as a side dish

For the dressing
1 tbsp olive oil
1 tbsp balsamic vinegar
1 tbsp lemon juice
1 tsp runny honey
½ tsp cumin seeds, dry-roasted
   in a small frying pan
Salt and pepper

For the salad
Cooking oil spray
250g young yellow courgettes,
   sliced lengthways into 2mm-
   thick ribbons
50g whole blanched almonds
75g baby herb salad leaves

Mix dressing ingredients and set aside. Heat the oil in a griddle pan and sauté the courgette slices and almonds for 2-3 minutes. Combine warm courgettes, almonds and leaves and add dressing. Season and serve.

OPTIONAL EXTRA: add a crumble of feta for tang and extra protein (+25 cals per tbsp).

...Puy lentil, orange and hazelnut

358 CALORIES PER PORTION

Serves 2

For the dressing
1 tbsp olive oil
1 tbsp balsamic vinegar
2 tbsp orange juice
1 garlic clove, very finely
  chopped
Salt and pepper

For the salad
1 250g pouch ready-to-eat Puy
  lentils
½ red onion, finely chopped
1 large carrot, peeled and grated
30g roasted chopped hazelnuts
Generous handful of curly
  parsley, chopped
1 tbsp orange zest, to serve

Combine oil, vinegar, orange juice, garlic, salt and pepper in a small bowl. Microwave the lentils in the pouch for 1 minute, then add to the bowl and stir in the red onion, carrot, hazelnuts and parsley. Mix well and serve at room temperature, scattered with orange zest.

OPTIONAL EXTRA: top each portion with 40g cubed marinated tofu for a more substantial supper (+60 cals). As an alternative, replace the carrot with a handful of chopped DIY oven-dried tomatoes, P161.

HOW TO STUFF A MUSHROOM...

Eating mushrooms in place of red meat can significantly slash your calorie intake, so swap them when you can. A big field mushroom works well as transport for veggies and punchy flavours, and all of these recipes will make a filling midweek supper. If you can't get a big field mushroom, two smaller Portobello mushrooms would work just as well.

...with spinach, chilli and cheese

173 CALORIES PER PORTION

Serves 1

Cooking oil spray
½ small red onion, finely
  chopped
1 small garlic clove, finely
  chopped
Pinch of chilli flakes

100g baby spinach leaves
1 large field mushroom, cleaned
  and trimmed
1 tsp olive oil
1 tbsp breadcrumbs
1 tbsp grated Parmesan

Preheat oven to 180°C. Heat a small pan, spray with oil and gently fry the red onion, garlic and chill flakes until softened. Add spinach, stir and cook gently until wilted. Drizzle mushroom with olive oil and season well. Spoon spinach mixture into the caps. Sprinkle with breadcrumbs and Parmesan, then bake for 15-20 minutes and serve.

...with goat's cheese and walnut

275 CALORIES PER PORTION

Serves 1

1 large field mushroom, cleaned
    and trimmed, stalk removed
    and chopped
50g soft goat's cheese

1 tbsp low-fat natural yoghurt
1 tbsp walnuts, chopped
1 tsp fresh thyme leaves
Salt and pepper

Preheat oven to 180°C. Combine chopped mushroom stalk with the
cheese, yoghurt, walnuts and thyme. Season mushroom cap and fill with
cheese mix. Bake for 15-20 minutes and serve.

FAST DAY TIP: goat's cheese is lower in calories than
cheese made from cow's milk, though this recipe also
works well with crumbled Stilton.

...pesto, pine nut and ricotta

283 CALORIES PER PORTION

Serves 1

1 large field mushroom, cleaned
and trimmed, stalk removed
and chopped
1 spring onion, chopped
Zest of half a lemon
1 tsp lemon juice

1 tbsp pesto sauce
50g ricotta cheese
1 tbsp pine nuts
Salt and pepper
Fresh basil leaves, to serve

Preheat oven to 180°C. Combine chopped mushroom stalk with the spring onion, lemon zest and juice, pesto, pine nuts and ricotta and mix well. Season the mushroom and spoon pesto mix into the cap, then bake in a small roasting tray for 15-20 minutes. Serve topped with basil leaves.

OPTIONAL EXTRA: add a handful of finely chopped rehydrated porcini mushrooms to the pesto mix for extra earthiness.

THE BEST LENTIL DAHL

203 CALORIES PER PORTION

Serves 6 as a side dish

Cook it long and slow, following each step for the necessary build-up of complex flavours. Find a consistency which suits you – thick, thin, your choice – or add more stock for dahl soup.

300g chana dahl (yellow dried split peas), rinsed
1.2l water
1 vegetable stock cube
1 tbsp sunflower oil
1 tbsp cumin seeds
1 onion, diced
3 green chillies, slit in half
2cm piece fresh root ginger, peeled and julienned

3 garlic cloves, peeled and left whole
3 tomatoes
2 tsp ground turmeric
1 tsp garam masala
1 tsp ground coriander
1 tsp lemon juice
100ml water
Salt and pepper
Handful of parsley, chopped, to serve

Place lentils and water in a pan with the vegetable stock cube, stir and bring to the boil. Skim off any froth – be sure to do this or the dahl will be bitter. Cover and reduce heat. Simmer, stirring regularly, for 35-40 minutes, or until the lentils are just tender, adding more water as necessary. Meanwhile, heat oil in another pan over a medium heat. Add cumin seeds and fry for 20-30 seconds, then add the onion, chillies and ginger and fry for 3-4 minutes. Blitz garlic and tomatoes in a food processor and add purée to the pan, stirring well to combine. Add the ground spices, lemon juice and a further 100ml water and stir well. Simmer for 5 minutes, then stir this spiced mix into the cooked lentils, adding more water if necessary. Cook for a further 10 minutes. Check seasoning – you may want to add a little salt once the lentils are cooked through (adding it earlier may make them tough). Serve with plenty of chopped parsley.

WHAT TO DO WITH A TIN OF BEANS...

...smashed cannellini with chilli and olives

226 CALORIES PER PORTION

Serves 2 as a side dish

1 400g tin cannellini beans,
  rinsed and drained
2 garlic cloves, peeled and left
  whole
1 dried chilli
1 sprig of sage
4 tbsp water

Salt and pepper
2 tsp lemon juice
2 tsp olive oil
1 tsp chilli flakes
50g small black pitted olives
100g baby spinach leaves

Heat beans, garlic, chilli, sage and water in a pan. Season and cook for
3 minutes. Remove garlic, chilli and sage, then mash the beans roughly
with a fork. Season well, add lemon juice, olive oil, chilli flakes, olives and
spinach. Stir and serve.

...white beans with pesto

254 CALORIES PER PORTION

Serves 2 as a side dish

Cooking oil spray
1 onion, finely chopped
1 garlic clove, crushed
1 bay leaf
1 400g tin haricot beans,
  rinsed and drained

2 tbsp pesto sauce
Salt and pepper
Lemon wedges and basil
  leaves, to serve

Heat a small frying pan and spray with oil. Fry the onion, garlic and bay leaf for 3 minutes on a medium heat until softened. Add beans and heat through. Remove from heat and add pesto sauce. Season and stir well to combine. Serve with lemon wedges and a handful of basil leaves.

...big baked beans

265 CALORIES PER PORTION

Serves 2 as a side dish

Cooking oil spray
1 onion, finely chopped
1 400g tin butter beans, rinsed
  and drained
2 tbsp tomato purée

½ tsp chilli flakes
1 tsp paprika
1 200g tin chopped tomatoes
1 tsp dried mixed herbs

Heat a pan and spray with oil and sauté onion until softened. Stir in the rest of the ingredients and simmer for 10 minutes, then serve.

...sweet and spiced coconut butter beans

316 CALORIES PER PORTION

Serves 2 as a side dish

2 tsp olive oil
1 tsp mustard seeds
4 dried curry leaves
1 onion, finely chopped
1 tbsp desiccated coconut
1 tsp ground turmeric
½ tsp ground ginger
1 red chilli, deseeded and finely sliced

2 ripe tomatoes, cored and finely chopped
1 tbsp mango chutney
Salt and pepper
1 400g tin butter beans, rinsed and drained
2 tsp lemon juice
100g baby spinach

Heat oil in a frying pan, add mustard seeds and fry for 1 minute. Add curry leaves, onion, coconut, turmeric, ginger and chilli and cook until onion has softened. Add tomato, mango chutney, salt and pepper and cook for a further 3 minutes. Stir in the butter beans with the lemon juice and continue to cook until they are heated through. Remove from heat and add spinach leaves. Combine and serve when spinach has just wilted.

FATOUSH SALAD

242 CALORIES PER PORTION

Serves 4 as a side dish

For the salad
1 large romaine lettuce, roughly chopped
3 ripe tomatoes, roughly chopped (and skinned if you prefer)
1 cucumber, peeled, deseeded and chopped
1 red onion, finely sliced
1 green pepper, deseeded and chopped
12 radishes, halved
12 black olives, pitted and chopped
Generous handful of curly parsley, chopped
Handful of mint leaves, chopped
Handful of dill, chopped
2 wholemeal pitta breads, toasted and torn into bite-sized pieces

For the dressing
2 tbsp olive oil
1 tbsp Dijon mustard
2 tbsp white wine vinegar
1 garlic clove, finely crushed
Salt and cracked black pepper

For the lemon-yoghurt sauce
150g low-fat natural yoghurt
1 tbsp tahini
1 tbsp lemon juice
Zest of half a lemon
½ tsp dried basil
½ tsp sumac
Salt and pepper

Handful of chopped herbs and 1 tbsp seeds to serve – choose from sunflower, sesame, mustard, poppy, pumpkin, or use a mix

Place the salad ingredients in a large bowl. Prepare dressing by combining all ingredients and whisking well to emulsify. In a separate bowl, mix the ingredients for the yoghurt sauce. Pour the dressing over the salad ingredients, toss well, then drizzle the yoghurt sauce on top. Add a scatter of seeds and serve with a final flourish of chopped herbs.

WHAT TO PUT IN A PEPPER...

Think of a pepper as a vessel for flavour and texture; the red and yellow varieties tend to be sweeter than the green.

...Puy lentil and porcini

247 CALORIES PER PORTION

Serves 1

Cooking oil spray
½ red onion, diced
1 garlic clove, crushed
10g porcini mushrooms,
    rehydrated in boiling water,
    drained and chopped,
    reserving 50ml mushroom
    water

100g ready-to-eat Puy lentils
Pinch of dried thyme, or 1 tsp
    fresh thyme leaves
1 pepper, halved and deseeded
1 tsp olive oil
Salt and pepper

Preheat oven to 180°C. Heat a small pan, lightly spray with oil and sauté onion until softened. Add garlic, stir and cook for a further minute. Add porcini, stir and cook for 2 minutes, then add lentils, thyme and 50ml of mushroom water. Season well, and heat through. Place the halved pepper in a small roasting tray, drizzle with a little olive oil and bake for 10 minutes. Add lentil mix, check seasoning and bake for a further 10-15 minutes.

...feta, tomato and chickpea

342 CALORIES PER PORTION

Serves 1

Cooking oil spray
1 spring onion, finely sliced
½ tsp paprika
200g canned chickpeas, rinsed
  and drained
1 ripe tomato, chopped

1 tbsp lemon juice
50g feta, crumbled
1 tbsp parsley, chopped
Salt and pepper
1 pepper, halved and deseeded
1 tsp olive oil

Preheat oven to 180°C. Heat a small pan, lightly spray with oil and sauté spring onion until softened. Add paprika, stir and cook for another minute. Remove from heat. Add chickpeas, tomato, lemon juice, feta and parsley, and season well. Place the halved pepper in a small roasting tray, drizzle with a little olive oil and bake for 10 minutes. Add the chickpea mix and bake for a further 10-15 minutes.

BUTTERNUT SQUASH WITH ROSEMARY AND LIME

260 CALORIES PER PORTION

Serves 2 as a side dish

1 small butternut squash,
   peeled, deseeded and cut
   into 2cm chunks
1 tbsp olive oil

Juice of a lime
2 tsp fresh rosemary leaves,
   finely chopped
Salt and pepper

Preheat oven to 180°C. Arrange butternut in a roasting tin, dress with oil, lime juice, rosemary, salt and pepper. Bake for 30 minutes, turning once during cooking time.

OPTIONAL EXTRA: serve with steamed broccoli florets, roasted pumpkin seeds (+60 cals per tbsp) and a crumble of feta (+50 cals).

● goes well with beef and beer casserole, P93.

A HOST OF GOOD THINGS TO SLING ON LEAVES OR GREENS

A simple leaf salad can be transformed into a more interesting and substantial supper with the addition of protein, colour and crunch. Try adding any of the following (all calorie counts are for 50g unless otherwise stated).

- lemon-dressed beansprouts +14
- bamboo shoots, water chestnuts and beansprouts +15
- thinly sliced red onion, celeriac or fennel +15
- steamed broccoli florets and pickled ginger +18
- shredded carrot and courgette 'noodles' +20
- edamame beans +30
- 1 tbsp of pecans or walnuts +50
- 1 tbsp of roasted seeds or pine nuts +58
- marinated tofu cubes +70
- 6 orange segments +25 and a tbsp of hazelnuts +50
- hard-boiled egg, +80 per medium egg, or quail's eggs
- 1 fresh fig +30 and torn half-fat mozzarella +80
- DIY oven-dried tomatoes +125
- goat's cheese +130 and blueberries (excellent with spinach leaves) +24
- cooked chickpeas +170
- crumbled Stilton +150 and pear slices +50

THE FAST DAY DRESSING

112 CALORIES PER TBSP

...the only one you really need.

1 tbsp lemon juice
1 tbsp white wine vinegar
2 tbsp olive oil
2 tsp Dijon mustard

1 garlic clove, peeled and left
  whole
Salt and pepper

Whisk all the ingredients together and keep in an air-tight jar in the fridge. It will last for a week. Remove the garlic clove before eating.

● try this dressing with flavoured vinegars.

FAST DAY TIP: extra-virgin olive oil is heart-friendly and will give you the best taste in a dressing. Most oils clock up 120 calories per tablespoon, so use sparingly – perhaps just a teaspoon. If you are rationing those Fast Day calories, consider dressing your salad with just a dash of balsamic vinegar. It's only 14 calories per tablespoon.

CORIANDER AND CHILLI DIPPING SAUCE

19 CALORIES PER TBSP

3 garlic cloves
1 tsp brown sugar
1 tsp galangal or root ginger,
  peeled and sliced
½ tbsp tamarind paste

2 tsp lime juice
2 tbsp water
Fresh coriander leaves, chopped
2 small red chillies

Blitz in a food processor and serve a spoonful alongside grilled white fish or any simple dish that needs a bolt of fire.

A QUICK TOMATO COULIS

26 CALORIES PER PORTION

Serves 6 as a sauce on the side

Less calorific than shop-bought sauces, which tend to have hidden sugars and preservatives. Make a batch and freeze in Fast Day portions.

1 400g tin chopped cherry
  tomatoes
2 tbsp tomato purée
½ tsp runny honey

Salt and pepper
2 tsp dried herb of choice –
  oregano or mixed herbs

Put ingredients in a small pan and simmer for 10 minutes to reduce. Blend for a smoother consistency.

DIY OVEN-DRIED TOMATOES

20 CALORIES PER 100G

This is one to make in high summer, when tomatoes are at their flavourful best.

20 ripe plum tomatoes
Sea salt
6 garlic cloves, crushed
3 tbsp fresh oregano, chopped

1 tbsp dried oregano
2 tbsp extra-virgin olive oil
1 tsp caster sugar
Freshly ground black pepper

Preheat oven to 120°C. Slice the tomatoes in half and scoop out the seeds. Salt well – a coarse salt works best here – and place, cut side down, on a wire rack or kitchen paper. Leave for 30 minutes, then rinse and dry. In a small bowl, combine the garlic, oreganos, olive oil, sugar and black pepper and dot the mix on the tomato halves. Place tomatoes on a wire rack over a roasting tray and bake in a very low oven for 3 hours, checking occasionally. Cool and store in an air-tight container in the fridge. They'll last for 2-3 weeks.

Supper soups

Warm. And wise

Soup is quick to make and brilliantly satiating, an all-round glory that is sometimes overlooked as we reach for a meat-and-two-veg meal. A decent stock is essential – without it your soup will almost certainly let you down. What you really need on a Fast Day is an honest, nourishing soup, preferably with some protein in it (beans and lentils will do the trick). For these calorie-controlled soups, I have skimmed off as much fat as possible and turned up the dial on taste.

STOCKY BROTH: THE WORLD'S EASIEST SOUP

VIRTUALLY NIL CALORIES

Have stock handy in the freezer; simply heat it up and add plenty of frozen veggies or herbs and you've got yourself a bowl of Fast Day flavour.

A few stock tips:

● Roasting bones before adding them to the stock pot will boost colour and flavour; a roasted chicken carcass is ideal.

● Don't chuck lone bones: freeze them and make a stock when you have a quantity

● Along with carrot, celery and onion, add bouquet garni for herby depth

● Adding a teaspoon of vinegar to a stock will aid the extraction of minerals without unduly influencing the flavour

● Don't salt a stock; season the final dish instead to avoid over-salting

● Once brought to a boil and skimmed, simmer slowly – a good stock should not be rushed or it will turn cloudy

● Vegetable stock generally has a lower fat content than chicken stock

● Once strained, be sure to skim off any fat and froth that rises to the top of the pot. Place kitchen roll on the surface to absorb oils, or chill first to make skimming easier

● If keeping a stock for later use, retain the layer of fat on top to protect it in the fridge. Simply skim when you're ready to use

● If you are freezing stock, boil the strained stock down in order to reduce it by about half. This will condense the flavour and save freezer space; add water when ready to use

What to add to the basic broth:

VEG: sugar snaps, mange touts, broccoli florets, edamame beans, baby spinach, a handful of herbs, spring onions, bamboo shoots, flageolet beans, peas, sweetcorn, French beans.

PROTEIN: strips of chicken breast, prawns, tofu. Or add a handful of dried porcini or ceps (rehydrate by soaking in boiling water for 30 minutes to make them plump; add the resulting liquor water to the stock for extra oomph). 100g dried porcini mushrooms has 26 calories and no fat, so they're a great Fast Day standby. Or try 'dried mixed forest mushrooms' for further depth.

FLAVOUR: if you're not adding fat, you do need to incorporate flavour from elsewhere. Add miso, stock cubes or bouillon powder to capitalise on taste. Then play around with herbs, spices, chillies, fish sauce, lime juice – whatever it takes to make a soup sing.

And to turn it into a satisfying Fast Day soup...

● favour clear vegetable broths. Miso soup and pho, for instance, are lower in calories than dense chowders, bisques and cream soups

● thicken stock with pulses rather than potatoes as they are lower GI. A handful of lentils should be adequate, or a tin of cannellini beans, blitzed or mashed once hot

● make soup in generous batches and freeze – smooth, thick soups tend to freeze best – and remember that soups, like stews, often taste better the next day

● when making a soup base, don't sweat onions in butter; use water or a scant spray of oil

WATERCRESS AND COURGETTE SOUP WITH PARMESAN AND PINE NUTS

126 CALORIES PER PORTION

Serves 4

1 tbsp olive oil
1 large onion, diced
500g courgettes, chopped
1 garlic clove, crushed
50g potatoes, peeled and
   chopped
1.25l vegetable stock

200g watercress, thicker stems
   removed
1 tbsp pine nuts
Salt and pepper
1 tbsp grated Parmesan
Fresh basil leaves

Heat oil in a large pan, add onion and sauté till softened but not coloured. Add courgettes, potatoes and garlic, sweat for 10 minutes, then add stock. Simmer for a further 10 minutes, partially covered, adding watercress for final 3 minutes. Meanwhile, dry-fry the pine nuts and set aside. Blitz the soup with a hand-blender, adjust consistency by adding extra water or stock if necessary, and season. Reheat and serve with a scatter of Parmesan, pine nuts and fresh basil leaves.

OPTIONAL EXTRA: serve topped with a soft poached egg instead of Parmesan and pine nuts.

EGG-DROP SOUP

161 CALORIES PER PORTION

Serves 2

This soup is simplicity itself, but it does rely on a decent stock, so go for the best you can get – either home-made or shop-bought in a pouch.

1.2l good, flavourful chicken stock, skimmed of fat
2 eggs
Salt and pepper

2 spring onions, finely chopped
Handful of fresh flat-leaf parsley, roughly chopped

Heat the stock till just simmering. Whisk eggs in a small bowl, season with a pinch of salt and pepper, add 1 tbsp water and then pour in a slow, thin stream into the gently simmering broth, stirring as you go to create elegant silken strands. Serve immediately, topped with a scatter of parsley and spring onion. For an Italian take on egg-drop soup, make stracciatella by adding 1 tbsp grated Parmesan, 1 tsp lemon zest, 1 tsp freshly chopped marjoram and a little nutmeg to the egg mix before the drop (add 20 cals for the Parmesan).

OPTIONAL EXTRA: add a handful or two of frozen peas and some baby spinach leaves to hot stock, then bring back to a simmer before adding egg.

TOM YUM

173 CALORIES PER PORTION

Serves 2

1.2l good chicken or vegetable
stock
1 tsp shrimp paste
1 lemon grass stalk, bruised
2 kaffir lime leaves
2cm fresh root ginger or
galangal, peeled and sliced
Small handful of coriander,
including stalks, chopped
1 whole chilli, halved and
deseeded
150g raw king prawns or squid
rings (fresh or frozen)

2 spring onions, finely sliced on
the diagonal
Handful of pak choi, sliced
100g green beans, blanched
10 cherry tomatoes, halved
1 tbsp mirin
1 tbsp Thai fish sauce
1 tbsp soy sauce
1 tbsp lime juice
½ tsp palm sugar or light
muscovado sugar
Coriander leaves, red chilli and
lime zest, to serve

In a large pan, heat stock, shrimp paste, lemon grass, lime leaves,
ginger, coriander and chilli. Simmer for 15 minutes then strain and return
the clear broth to the pan. Reheat and add prawns or squid (or both),
together with the spring onions. Simmer for a further 3 minutes. Add
pak choi, beans, tomatoes, mirin, fish sauce, soy sauce, lime juice and
sugar. Continue to simmer for 2-3 minutes or until the vegetables are just
tender. Serve sprinkled with coriander leaves, a little more red chilli and a
grating of lime zest.

● this also works well with 150g chicken breast fillet,
cut into thin strips and added to the hot stock.

OPTIONAL EXTRA: try adding some shiitake
mushrooms, bamboo shoots, silken tofu or edamame.

EASY PEA AND HAM

228 CALORIES PER PORTION

Serves 4

1 tsp butter
1l ham or chicken stock,
   skimmed of fat
1 onion, diced
1 medium-sized potato, peeled
   and diced

1 ham or chicken stock cube
500g frozen petits pois
200g thick sliced ham, trimmed
   of any fat and diced
Salt and pepper

Heat the butter and 2 tbsp of the stock in a saucepan and gently sweat the onion until translucent. Add the potato, the rest of the stock and the stock cube, then simmer for 10 minutes. Add the peas and bring back to a simmer for 2-3 minutes. Remove from the heat and blitz with a hand blender until smooth. Stir in the diced ham, adjust seasoning if necessary (the stock cube and ham may make the soup salty enough already). Serve, perhaps in a mug, on a cold day.

CRAB AND CORN CHOWDER

248 CALORIES PER PORTION

Serves 4

1 onion, finely diced
1 leek, trimmed and finely
  chopped
2 celery sticks, finely chopped
2 carrots, peeled and finely
  chopped
1l chicken or vegetable stock
2 medium potatoes, peeled and
  diced

200g frozen sweetcorn
170g tin white crabmeat,
  drained
3 tbsp half-fat crème fraîche
Salt and pepper
Chives and nutmeg, to serve

Place the onion, leek, celery and carrots in a large pan and add a few tablespoons of the stock. Sweat over a medium heat for about 10 minutes, stirring regularly until soft and taking care that it doesn't stick (add a dash more stock if it threatens to). Add the potatoes and the remainder of the stock, stir, and simmer for 10-15 minutes or until the potato is tender. Add the sweetcorn and crabmeat, then simmer for a further 3 minutes. Remove from the heat, stir in the crème fraîche and season well with plenty of freshly milled black pepper. Serve with a scatter of snipped chives and a grate of nutmeg.

OPTIONAL EXTRA: for a deeper, richer flavour, add 100g diced pancetta to the onions as they fry (+100 cals per portion). Or make a curried version by adding 2 tsp curry powder along with the potatoes.

PISTOU

284 CALORIES FOR THE BROTH + 117 FOR THE PISTOU

Serves 2

Pistou is a Provençal sauce made from garlic and basil. The Argentines make a similar sauce called chimichurri, which relies on parsley and chilli. But the point of these – and of pesto – is the same: a whack of flavour. Here, pistou wakes up a good veggie broth. But you could just as well serve it alongside plain grilled chicken or steak.

For the broth
Cooking oil spray
1 onion, finely diced
1 large leek, trimmed and finely
  sliced
1 fennel bulb, finely chopped
2 carrots, peeled and finely
  chopped
2 courgettes, finely chopped
1 bay leaf
1 celery stick, finely chopped
1 tbsp fresh parsley, chopped
1 400g tin borlotti or
  cannellini beans, rinsed and
  drained

1 400g tin chopped tomatoes
500ml chicken or vegetable
  stock
Salt and pepper
Lemon zest, to serve

For the pistou sauce
3 garlic cloves
Small handful of fresh basil
  leaves
2 tbsp olive oil
60g Parmesan, grated
½ tsp sea salt

Spray a large saucepan with oil and sauté the onion and leek for 3-4 minutes over a medium heat, stirring and adding a spoonful or two of stock if they stick. Add all the other broth ingredients to the pan, stir, season lightly and simmer until the vegetables are tender – about 15 minutes. For the pistou sauce, put the ingredients in a blender and pulse to a smooth paste. Serve the hot soup in a deep bowl with a dollop of pistou and a final grating of lemon zest.

BUTTERNUT SQUASH WITH SPICED SAFFRON YOGHURT

285 CALORIES PER PORTION

Serves 4

1kg butternut squash, peeled, deseeded and chopped

500g tomatoes, quartered and cored (and skinned if you wish)

2 garlic cloves, peeled

2 carrots, peeled and chopped

1 onion, chopped

1 tbsp olive oil

1 tsp dried chilli flakes

2 star anise

2 tsp ground cumin

2 tsp ground coriander

2 tsp paprika

Salt and pepper

1.5l vegetable stock

100g red lentils

For the spiced yoghurt

150g low-fat natural yoghurt

Small pinch of saffron threads

1 tsp cumin seeds

1 tsp ground cumin

Generous pinch of fresh sage leaves, and 1 tbsp toasted pumpkin seeds (optional), to serve

Preheat oven to 180°C. Place the butternut squash, tomatoes, garlic, carrots and onion in a roasting pan and drizzle with oil. Add spices, season and mix well, then cover with foil and bake until everything is tender – about an hour. Remove star anise from the pan. In a large saucepan, roughly mash the baked vegetables and stir in the stock. Bring to a simmer, then add lentils and cook on a low heat for 20 minutes. Season, adding a little extra stock if the soup is too thick. If you prefer a smoother soup, blitz with a hand blender; for supreme silkiness, you could even pass it through a sieve and reheat. Combine the spiced yoghurt ingredients in a bowl, stirring well to release the saffron's golden colour. Serve the soup in deep bowls with a swirled spoonful of spiced yoghurt, a handful of toasted pumpkin seeds (+75 cals per tbsp) and young sage leaves scattered on top.

GREEN TEA CHICKEN SOUP

377 CALORIES PER PORTION

Serves 4

The addition of green tea gives this pretty soup a subtle new flavour – expect delicate rather than bold. By all means, use ready-made stock and fresh chicken breast rather than cooking the bird whole to produce a fresh stock.

1 small chicken, washed and
  dried (approx. 1.2kg)
3 large leeks, trimmed and
  roughly chopped
4 carrots, peeled and chopped
1 onion, diced
3 celery sticks, chopped
3cm fresh root ginger, peeled
  and sliced
3 sprigs of fresh thyme
1 tsp peppercorns

2 bay leaves
1 chicken stock cube
300ml strong green tea, strained
  if loose leaf, or tea-bag
  removed
100g frozen petits pois
2 spring onions, finely sliced
Juice of a lemon
Salt and pepper
2 tbsp curly parsley, chopped,
  to serve

Place chicken in a large pan with the leeks, carrots, onion, celery and ginger. Add thyme, peppercorns and bay, then fill the pan with enough cold water to just cover the chicken. Bring to boil, then cover and simmer for 1½ hours. Remove chicken from the pan, set aside and strain the broth, skimming off any froth or fat. Return broth to the heat and add crumbled stock cube. Meanwhile, discard chicken skin and remove the meat from bones; shred and return to pan of broth, along with the green tea, peas and spring onions. Heat through for 3-4 minutes, then add lemon juice and season well. Serve sprinkled with fresh parsley – don't omit this, it's part of the delicate charm of the dish.

PRAWN LAKSA

400 CALORIES PER PORTION

Serves 2

This spiced Malaysian noodle soup is a proper meal in a bowl and has a fairly generous number of calories to match (but it's worth every last one of them).

150g fine rice noodles
2 tbsp laksa paste from a jar
400ml half-fat coconut milk
500ml chicken stock
2 spring onions, finely sliced
   on the diagonal, a few slices
   reserved for garnish
1 red chilli, halved and
   deseeded, finely sliced

100g prawns, fresh or cooked
100g beansprouts
1 pak choi, thinly sliced

¼ cucumber, peeled, deseeded
   and cut into fine strips, and a
   handful of fresh coriander
   leaves, to serve

Prepare noodles according to packet instructions and set aside. Heat a large pan, add the laksa paste and 1 tbsp coconut milk. Fry for 3 minutes to release the paste's flavour, then add the rest of the coconut milk, stock, spring onions and chilli. Stir, and simmer for 2 minutes. Add the prawns, beansprouts and pak choi and simmer for a further 3 minutes until the prawns and vegetables are just cooked. Check seasoning. Place the prepared noodles in bowls, and cover with the hot soup. Garnish with delicate strips of cucumber, a little more finely sliced spring onion and coriander leaves.

RECIPES BY CALORIE COUNT

Calories	Recipe	Page
0	Stocky broth	164
14	Lemon-dressed beansprouts (50g)	158
15	Bamboo shoots, water chestnuts and beansprouts (50g)	158
15	Sliced red onion, celeriac or fennel (50g)	158
18	Steamed broccoli florets (50g) and pickled ginger	158
19	Coriander and chilli dipping sauce	160
20	DIY oven-dried tomatoes	161
20	Roasted marrow, courgette and red onion wedges (100g)	23
20	Shredded carrot and courgette 'noodles' (50g)	158
25	Pan-fried chicory (100g)	122
25	Saffron and shallot sauce	81
27	Spring greens with mustard seeds	127
30	Edamame beans (50g)	158
35	Veg 'noodles' (100g)	25
36	Cauliflower 'couscous'	128
50	Tbsp of pecans or walnuts	158
58	Tbsp of roasted seeds or pine nuts	158
68	Saag on the side	129
70	Marinated tofu cubes (50g)	158
74	Chunky cumin coleslaw	130
75	6 orange segments and a tbsp of hazelnuts	158
79	Spiced red cabbage with apples	131
80	Hardboiled egg	158
92	Celeriac remoulade	132
105	Prawn and asparagus stir fry	46
110	Fresh fig and 50g torn half-fat mozzarella	158
112	The Fast Day dressing	159

Calories	Recipe	Page
123	Baked fennel with Parmesan and thyme	135
	Tabbouleh	133
124	Chunky cumin coleslaw with walnuts	130
125	DIY oven-dried tomatoes 50g	158
126	Watercress and courgette soup with Parmesan and pine nuts	166
128	Shoots and leaves red curry	74
133	Asian sesame salad	137
137	Monkfish curry	76
140	Chicken, gremolata and dark leaves	48
	Spiced brown lentils salad with mint	140
142	Cauliflower mash	138
144	Mexican blackbean chilli	21
150-190	Fast Day plain omelette	68
150-465	Fast Day omelette variations	68–9
154	Goat's cheese (50g) and blueberries (50g)	158
	Stuffed pepper with Puy lentils and porcini	154
161	Egg-drop soup	167
162	Chicken tagine with preserved lemons and saffron	78
163	Chicken in piri piri sauce	50
165	Prawn, asparagus, sweetcorn and sugar snaps stir fry	46
170	Cooked chickpeas (50g)	158
173	Stuffed mushroom with spinach, chilli and cheese	144
	Tom yum	168
	Turkey kofte with tzatziki (no pitta)	114
175	No-fuss fish with chilli dressing	55
179	Chicken, peppers and capers	51
	Neapolitan cianfotta (summer vegetable stew)	82
180	Borlotti-bean Bolognaise	26
	Skinny spag bol	25

Calories	Recipe	Page
	Cannellini bean mash	138–9
183	Simple seared sirloin	100
	Sweet potato and carrot mash	139
184	Warm chicken liver salad	57
200	Crumbled Stilton (50g) and pear slices (50g)	158
203	The best lentil dahl	147
207	One-pot bean feast	84
209	Quick Quorn chilli	22
210	Dijon marinated chicken	52
214	Mexican blackbean chilli with avocado	21
215	Garlic and parsley prawns	105
220	Borlotti-bean Bolognaise with olives	26
221	Chicken masala and raita	53
222	Ten-minute king prawn curry	106
226	Smashed cannellini with chilli and olives	148
228	Easy pea and ham soup	169
230	Chilli beef stir fry	107
233	Fast fish pie	27
234	Quick-fire burgers with hot tomato sauce	108
239	Coq au vin	28
241	Low-cal chilli con carne	23
242	Fatoush salad	153
244	Warm chicken liver salad with hazelnuts	57
247	Fire and spice veggie casserole	85
248	Crab and corn chowder	171
	Five-minute roast beef salad	59
249	Chickpea curry in a hurry	60
253	Yellow courgette and almond salad	141
254	White beans with pesto	149
260	Butternut squash with rosemary and lime	157

Calories	Recipe	Page
263	Lamb steaks with mushy peas	109
	A quick tomato coulis	160
	Sirloin steak, rocket and watercress with horseradish cream	100
265	Big baked beans	149
267	Easy lamb kebabs	111
273	Chinese spiced chicken	54
275	Hot paprika goulash	31
	Stuffed mushroom with goat's cheese and walnut	145
276	Smoked haddock gratin	33
278	Yellow courgette and almond salad with feta	141
279	Tandoori chicken with mint dip and saag on the side	34
280	Chickpea curry in a hurry with spinach or tomatoes	60
283	Huevos rancheros	112
	Stuffed mushroom with pesto, pine nut and ricotta	146
285	Butternut squash soup with spiced saffron yoghurt	174
287	Sirloin steak with pepper sauce	101
292	Sirloin steak with chilli dipping sauce and pak choi	101
294	Basic boeuf bourguignon	35
297	Fast Day fishcakes with Thai salad	36
299	Nut-brown rice	76
310	Turkey kofte with tzatziki and warm pitta	114
311	Vegetable tagine with herbed couscous	79
313	Sirloin steak with herb dressing	102
316	Sweet and spiced coconut butter beans	151
318	Chicken cassoulet	87
319	Chickpea curry in a hurry with almonds	60
	Madras beef with a tomato and red onion salad	115
323	Sirloin steak with busted tomatoes and olives	102
324	Garam masala tuna steak	61
328	Italian rabbit stew	89

Calories	Recipe	Page
331	Super-fast Thai green chicken curry	38
335	Panko 'fried' chicken	117
336	Fast Day fishcakes with Thai papaya salad	36
337	Fast Day biryani	39
342	Stuffed pepper with feta, tomato and chickpea	155
348	Chicken Provençal	90
348	Crab and corn chowder with pancetta	171
349	Moroccan spiced lamb tagine	81
358	Puy lentil, orange and hazelnut salad	142
360	Chilli beef stir fry with fresh egg noodles	107
360	Cottage pie	40
365	Smoked haddock and prawn gratin	33
368	Kashmiri chicken and yoghurt curry	91
370	Butternut squash with rosemary, lime, broccoli, pumpkin seeds and feta	157
377	Green tea chicken soup	177
380	Baked falafel with two dipping sauces	63
385	Sea bass with tomato, chorizo and butter beans	119
386	Quick roast pork loin with broccoli and cauliflower cheese	64
390	Moussaka	41
393	Fast fish pie with eggs	27
394	Chicken curry with lemongrass and ginger	92
396	Madras beef with a tomato and red onion salad and brown rice	115
397	Express kedgeree	43
398	Beef and beer casserole	93
400	Prawn laksa	179
401	Boston beans and ham	94
401	Pistou and broth	173
415	Sea bass with tomato, chorizo, butter beans and olives	119
418	Puy lentil, orange and hazelnut salad with tofu	142

Calories	Recipe	Page
423	Venison sausages with cannellini bean mash	120
429	Beef daube with peppered greens	96
467	Peppered pork with summer slaw	66
493	Peppered pork with warm winter slaw	67
501	Lamb in a pan	122
526	Lamb in a pan with pan-fried chicory	122
548	Huevos rancheros with avocado, chilli sauce and tortilla	112

INDEX

5:2 rules 10, 16

Alcohol 123
Almonds
  chickpea curry in a hurry 60
  yellow courgette and almond salad 141
Anchovy and caper dressing 122
Apples
  chunky cumin coleslaw 130
  peppered pork with summer slaw 66
  spiced red cabbage with apples 131
Asian sesame salad 137
Asparagus, prawn and asparagus stir fry 46
Aubergines
  easy lamb kebabs 111
  moussaka 41

Balsamic vinegar 159
Bamboos shoots, shoots and leaves red
  curry 74
Beans 12
  big baked beans 149
  borlotti-bean Bolognaise 26
  Boston beans and ham 94
  cannellini bean mash 120, 138–9
  chicken cassoulet 87
  low-cal chilli con carne 23
  Mexican blackbean chilli 21
  one-pot bean feast 84
  quick Quorn chilli 22
  sea bass with tomato, chorizo and butter
    beans 119
  smashed cannellini with chilli and olives 148
  sweet and spiced coconut butter beans 151
  venison sausages with cannellini bean
    mash 120
  white beans with pesto 149
Beansprouts
  Asian sesame salad 137
  prawn laksa 179
  shoots and leaves red curry 74
Beef
  basic boeuf bourguignon 35
  beef and beer casserole 93
  beef daube with peppered greens 96
  chilli beef stir fry 107
  cottage pie 40
  five-minute roast beef salad 59
  hot paprika goulash 31

low-cal chilli con carne 23
Madras beef with a tomato and red
  onion salad 115
simple seared sirloin and 5
  quick accompaniments 100–2
skinny spag bol 25
Beer, beef casserole 93
Big baked beans 149
Biryani 39
Blackbeans, Mexican chilli 21
Boeuf bourguignon 35
Bolognaise
  borlotti-bean Bolognaise 26
  skinny spag bol 25
Boston beans and ham 94
Breakfast ideas 11, 123
Broccoli, quick roast pork loin with broccoli
  and cauliflower cheese 64
Broth 164–5
Bulgur wheat, tabbouleh 133
Butter beans
  big baked beans 149
  sea bass with tomato, chorizo and butter
    beans 119
  sweet and spiced coconut butter beans 151
Butternut squash
  with rosemary and lime 157
  soup with spiced saffron yoghurt 174
  vegetable tagine with herbed couscous 79

Cabbage
  Asian sesame salad 137
  beef daube with peppered greens 96
  chunky cumin coleslaw 130
  peppered pork with summer slaw 66
  peppered pork with warm winter slaw 67
  spiced red cabbage with apples 131
  spring greens with mustard seeds 127
Calorie allowance 10, 17
Calorie count guidance for recipes 16
Cannellini beans
  mash 120, 138–9
  smashed with chilli and olives 148
Capers, chicken, peppers and capers 51
Carbohydrates 13
Carrots
  green tea chicken soup 177
  mash with sweet potato 139
Cashews, Asian sesame salad 137
Cauliflower
  'couscous' 128
  mash 138

quick roast pork loin with broccoli and
cauliflower cheese 64
Celeriac
chunky cumin coleslaw 130
cottage pie 40
remoulade 132
Chana dahl, the best 147
Cheese 12–13
baked fennel with Parmesan and thyme 135
moussaka 41
quick roast pork loin with broccoli and
cauliflower cheese 64
smoked haddock gratin 33
stuffed mushroom with goat's cheese and
walnut 145
stuffed mushroom with pesto, pine nut
and ricotta 146
stuffed mushroom with spinach, chilli and
cheese 144
stuffed pepper with feta, tomato and
chickpea 155
watercress and courgette soup with
Parmesan and pine nuts 166
Chicken
as alternative ingredient 89, 168
chicken cassoulet 87
chicken curry with lemongrass and ginger
92
chicken, gremolata and dark leaves 48
chicken in piri piri sauce 50
chicken masala and raita 53
chicken, peppers and capers 51
chicken Provençal 90
chicken tagine with preserved lemons
and saffron 78
Chinese spiced chicken 54
coq au vin 28
Dijon marinated chicken 52
Fast Day biryani 39
green tea chicken soup 177
Kashmiri chicken and yoghurt curry 91
panko 'fried' chicken 117
super-fast Thai green chicken curry 38
tandoori chicken with mint dip and saag
on the side 34
warm chicken liver salad 57
Chicken livers, warm chicken liver salad 57
Chickpeas 12
chickpea curry in a hurry 60
Moroccan spiced lamb tagine 81
stuffed pepper with feta, tomato and
chickpea 155

vegetable tagine with herbed couscous 79
Chicory, pan-fried 122
Chilli beef stir fry 107
Chilli con carne 23
Chinese spiced chicken 54
Chorizo
chicken cassoulet 87
sea bass with tomato, chorizo and butter
beans 119
Chowder, crab and corn 171
Coconut butter beans, sweet and spiced 151
Coleslaw
chunky cumin coleslaw 130
summer slaw 66
warm winter slaw 67
Coq au vin 28
Coriander and chilli dipping sauce 160
Cottage pie 40
Courgettes
roasted marrow, courgette and red onion
wedges 23
watercress and courgette soup with
Parmesan and pine nuts 166
yellow courgette and almond salad 141
Couscous
cauliflower 128
vegetable tagine with herbed couscous 79
Crab and corn chowder 171
Curries
the best lentil dahl 147
chicken curry with lemongrass and
ginger 92
chicken masala and raita 53
chickpea curry in a hurry 60
Fast Day biryani 39
garam masala tuna steak 61
Kashmiri chicken and yoghurt curry 91
monkfish curry 76
prawn laksa 179
shoots and leaves red curry 74
super-fast Thai green chicken curry 38
sweet and spiced coconut butter beans 151
ten-minute king prawn curry 106

Dahl, the best lentil 147
Dairy produce 12–13
Dijon marinated chicken 52
DIY oven-dried tomatoes 161
Dressings 13, 14
anchovy and caper 122
chilli 55
Fast Day dressing 159

fatoush 153
herb 102
honey and cumin 141
mint 140
remoulade 132
sesame 137
for warm winter slaw 67
Drinks 16, 123

Eggs 12
egg-drop soup 167
express kedgeree 43
Fast Day omelette with variations 68–9
fast fish pie 27
huevos rancheros 112
Express kedgeree 43

Falafel with two dipping sauces 63
Fantastic Five 14
Fast Day dressing 159
Fast Day rules 10, 16
Fasting benefits 10–11
Fatoush salad 153
Fats 13
Fennel
baked with Parmesan and thyme 135
remoulade 132
Fire and spice veggie casserole 85
Fish
as alternative ingredient 38
express kedgeree 43
fast day fishcakes with Thai salad 36
fast fish pie 27
garam masala tuna steak 61
monkfish curry 76
no-fuss fish with chilli dressing 55
sea bass with tomato, chorizo and
butter beans 119
smoked haddock gratin 33
Five-minute roast beef salad 59
Flavour boosting 13–14
Fridge and freezer staples 14–15

Garam masala tuna steak 61
Garlic and parsley prawns 105
Garlic, roasted 12–13
Goulash 31
Green beans
tom yum 168
warm chicken liver salad 57
Green tea chicken soup 177
Gremolata 48

Ham
with Boston beans 94
easy pea and ham soup 169
Hazelnuts, Puy lentil, orange and
hazelnut salad 142
Herbs 13
dressing 102
tabbouleh 133
Horseradish cream 100
Hot paprika goulash 31
Huevos rancheros 112
Hunger pangs 17

Italian rabbit stew 89

Kale, beef daube with peppered greens 96
Kashmiri chicken and yoghurt curry 91
Kebabs, easy lamb 111
Kedgeree 43
Kidney beans
low-cal chilli con carne 23
quick Quorn chilli 22

Lamb
easy lamb kebabs 111
lamb in a pan 122
lamb steaks with mushy peas 109
Moroccan spiced lamb tagine 81
moussaka 41
quick-fire burgers with hot tomato sauce
108
Larder staples 15
Leeks
cottage pie 40
green tea chicken soup 177
Lemons 14
chicken tagine with preserved lemons
and saffron 78
lemon-yoghurt sauce 153
Lentils 12
the best lentil dahl 147
fire and spice veggie casserole 85
moussaka 41
Puy lentil, orange and hazelnut salad 142
spiced brown lentils salad with mint 140
stuffed pepper with Puy lentils and
porcini 154
Liver, warm chicken liver salad 57

Madras beef with a tomato and red onion
salad 115
Mange tout, chilli beef stir fry 107

Marrow, courgette and red onion wedges, roasted 23
Meat 12
Mexican blackbean chilli 21
Monkfish curry 76
Moroccan spiced lamb tagine 81
Moussaka 41
Mushrooms 12
  beef and beer casserole 93
  chilli beef stir fry 107
  coq au vin 28
  easy lamb kebabs 111
  fire and spice veggie casserole 85
  Italian rabbit stew 89
  stuffed pepper with Puy lentils and porcini 154
  stuffed with goat's cheese and walnut 145
  stuffed with pesto, pine nut and ricotta 146
  stuffed with spinach, chilli and cheese 144
Mustard
  Dijon marinated chicken 52
  spring greens with mustard seeds 127

Neapolitan cianfotta (summer vegetable stew) 82
No-fuss fish with chilli dressing 55
Noodles
  prawn laksa 179
  shirataki 13
Nut-brown rice 76
Nuts 12, 15
  Asian sesame salad 137
  chickpea curry in a hurry 60
  nut-brown rice 76
  Puy lentil, orange and hazelnut salad 142
  shoots and leaves red curry 74
  stuffed mushroom with goat's cheese and walnut 145
  stuffed mushroom with pesto, pine nut and ricotta 146
  vegetable tagine with herbed couscous 79
  watercress and courgette soup with Parmesan and pine nuts 166
  yellow courgette and almond salad 141

Oats 11, 13
Oils 13
Olives
  borlotti-bean Bolognaise 26
  sea bass with tomato, chorizo, butter beans 119
  sirloin steak with busted tomatoes and olives 102
  smashed cannellini with chilli and olives 148
Omelette with variations 68–9
One-pot bean feast 84
Onions
  Madras beef with a tomato and red onion salad 115
  roasted marrow, courgette and red onion wedges 23
  sautéing 13
Oranges, Puy lentil, orange and hazelnut salad 142

Pak choi
  Asian sesame salad 137
  prawn laksa 179
  sirloin steak with chilli dipping sauce and pak choi 101
  tom yum 168
Pancetta
  coq au vin 28
  crab and corn chowder 171
Panko 'fried' chicken 117
Papaya, fast day fishcakes with Thai salad 36
Peanuts, shoots and leaves red curry 74
Peas
  chilli beef stir fry 107
  easy pea and ham soup 169
  lamb steaks with mushy peas 109
Pepper sauce 101
Peppered pork
  with summer slaw 66
  with warm winter slaw 67
Peppers
  chicken, peppers and capers 51
  chicken Provençal 90
  easy lamb kebabs 111
  stuffed with feta, tomato and chickpea 155
  stuffed with Puy lentils and porcini 154
Pesto
  stuffed mushroom with pesto, pine nut and ricotta 146
  white beans with pesto 149
Pine nuts
  stuffed mushroom with pesto, pine nut and ricotta 146
  vegetable tagine with herbed couscous 79
  watercress and courgette soup with Parmesan and pine nuts 166
Piri piri sauce 50
Pistou and broth 173
Pitta bread

baked falafel with two dipping sauces 63
fatoush salad 153
turkey kofte with tzatziki 114
Pork
  peppered pork with summer slaw 66
  peppered pork with warm winter slaw 67
  quick roast loin with broccoli and cauliflower
    cheese 64
Prawns
as alternative ingredient 38, 90
  fast fish pie 27
  garlic and parsley prawns 105
  prawn and asparagus stir fry 46
  prawn laksa 179
  smoked haddock and prawn gratin 33
  ten-minute king prawn curry 106
  tom yum 168
Protein 12
Puy lentils
  salad with orange and hazelnuts 142
  stuffed pepper with Puy lentils and porcini
    154

Quick-fire burgers with hot tomato sauce 108
Quick no-cook ideas 70
Quorn, quick chilli 22

Rabbit, Italian rabbit stew 89
Raita 53
Rice 13
  express kedgeree 43
  Fast Day biryani 39
  nut-brown rice 76
Ricotta, stuffed mushroom with pesto,
  pine nut and ricotta 146
Rocket, sirloin steak, rocket and watercress
  with horseradish cream 100

Saag on the side 34, 129
Saffron and shallot sauce 81
Saffron yoghurt 174
Salads
  Asian sesame salad 137
  fatoush salad 153
  five-minute roast beef salad 59
  Madras beef with a tomato and red
    onion salad 115
  Puy lentil, orange and hazelnut salad 142
  simple salad ideas 158
  spiced brown lentils salad with mint 140
  Thai salad 36
  warm chicken liver salad 57

yellow courgette and almond salad 141
Salmon
  as alternative ingredient 38
  fast day fishcakes with Thai salad 36
Satiety 12
Sauces
  cannellini bean dip 139
  chilli dipping sauce 101
  coriander and chilli dipping 160
  gremolata 48
  horseradish cream 100
  lemon-yoghurt 153
  mint dip 34
  pepper 101
  piri piri 50
  pistou 173
  quick tomato coulis 160
  raita 53
  saffron and shallot 81
  tomato 108
  tzatziki 114
Sausages, venison, with cannellini bean
  mash 120
Sea bass with tomato, chorizo and
  butter beans 119
Sesame dressing 137
Shirataki noodles 13
Shoots and leaves red curry 74
Sirloin steak, see steak
Skinny spag bol 25
Smashed cannellini with chilli and olives 148
Smoked haddock
  fast fish pie 27
  gratin 33
Smoked mackerel, express kedgeree 43
Snacks 16, 123
Soup
  butternut squash soup with spiced
    saffron yoghurt 174
  crab and corn chowder 171
  easy pea and ham soup 169
  egg-drop soup 167
  pistou and broth 173
  stocky broth 164–5
  tom yum 168
  watercress and courgette soup with
    Parmesan and pine nuts 166
Spiced brown lentils salad with mint 140
Spiced red cabbage with apples 131
Spinach
  chickpea curry in a hurry 60
  fast fish pie 27

saag on the side 34, 129
shoots and leaves red curry 74
smoked haddock gratin 33
stuffed mushroom with spinach, chilli
    and cheese 144
tandoori chicken with mint dip and saag
    on the side 34
ten-minute king prawn curry 106
Spring greens
beef daube with peppered greens 96
    with mustard seeds 127
Squid, tom yum 168
Steak
with busted tomatoes and olives 102
with chilli dipping sauce and pak choi 101
with herb dressing 102
with pepper sauce 101
with rocket and watercress and horseradish
    cream 100
simple seared 100
Stocky broth 164
Straight to the plate ideas 70
Stuffed mushrooms 144–6
Stuffed peppers 154–5
Sweet and spiced coconut butter beans 151
Sweet potato and carrot mash 139
Sweetcorn, crab and corn chowder 171

Tabbouleh 133
Tagines
chicken tagine with preserved lemons and
    saffron 78
Moroccan spiced lamb tagine 81
vegetable tagine with herbed couscous 79
Takeaway options 123
Tandoori chicken with mint dip and saag
    on the side 34
Ten-minute king prawn curry 106
Thai green chicken curry 38
Tofu 12
as alternative ingredient 38
Puy lentil, orange and hazelnut salad 142
Tom yum 168
Tomatoes 14
big baked beans 149
chickpea curry in a hurry 60
DIY oven-dried tomatoes 161
huevos rancheros 112
Madras beef with a tomato and red onion
    salad 115
moussaka 41
quick-fire burgers with tomato sauce 108

quick tomato coulis 160
sea bass with tomato, chorizo and butter
    beans 119
sirloin steak with busted tomatoes and
    olives 102
stuffed pepper with feta, tomato and
    chickpea 155
Tuna, garam masala tuna steak 61
Turkey kofte with tzatziki and warm pitta 114
Tzatziki 114

Vegetables see also salads and entries under
    specific vegetables
fire and spice veggie casserole 85
Mexican blackbean chilli 21
Neapolitan cianfotta (summer vegetable
    stew) 82
pistou and broth 173
roasting 12
shoots and leaves red curry 74
variety 12
veg 'noodles' 25
vegetable tagine with herbed couscous 79
Venison sausages with cannellini bean
    mash 120

Walnuts
chunky cumin coleslaw 130
stuffed mushroom with goat's cheese
    and walnut 145
Warm chicken liver salad 57
Watercress
Asian sesame salad 137
sirloin steak, rocket and watercress with
horseradish cream 100
watercress and courgette soup with
    Parmesan and pine nuts 166
White beans with pesto 149

Yellow courgette and almond salad 141
Yoghurt 12
butternut squash soup with spiced saffron
    yoghurt 174
Kashmiri chicken and yoghurt curry 91
lemon-yoghurt sauce 153
mint dip 34
raita 53
saffron and shallot 81
tzatziki 114

Acknowledgements

Little did we know, when we first gathered at the Clerkenwell Kitchen on a chilly October day in 2012, that *The Fast Diet* would cause such an almighty stir. My thanks, heartfelt and constant, go to Aurea Carpenter and Rebecca Nicolson of Short Books. And, of course, to Dr Michael Mosley, who responded to the 3am text message that launched a diet phenomenon and changed the lives (and weight) of thousands.

I am ever grateful to Team Fast Diet: to Paul Bougourd, Emmie Francis, Klara Zak and Catherine Gibbs for their ceaseless energy, industry and support; to Georgia Vaux for her brilliant FD design; and to Annie Hudson, who watched over my recipes and made sure that they didn't stick or burn or contain too much chilli (I like it hot). Romas Foord's photos continue to make Fast food look fabulous. And I thank Nicola Jeal, again, because I'll never quite manage to say it enough.

A big thank you to my mum Marmalade, fount of culinary wisdom, for her help with *Fast Cook*. And finally, love ever to my sticky-fingered kids – Lily and Ned – and to PBQC. Now that he's on the *Fast Diet* too, he keeps telling me how many calories are in a biscuit. Which is, y'know, quite annoying...

Mimi Spencer has written about body shape, diet and food trends in national newspapers and magazines for more than 20 years. She co-authored *The Fast Diet* (Short Books, 2013) with Dr Michael Mosley and wrote *The Fast Diet Recipe Book* (Short Books, 2013). @mimispencer1

photo by Craig Hibbert